THE WANANO INDIANS OF THE BRAZILIAN AMAZON

The Wanano Indians of the Brazilian Amazon: *A Sense of Space*

Janet M. Chernela

University of Texas Press, Austin

Requests for permission to reproduce material from this work
should be sent to Permissions, University of Texas Press, Box 7819,
Austin, TX 78713-7819.

ⓧ The paper used in this publication meets the minimum
requirements of American National Standard for Information
Sciences—Permanence of Paper for Printed Library Materials,
ANSI Z39.48-1984.

Library of Congress Cataloging-in-Publication Data
Chernela, Janet Marion, date.
    The Wanano Indians of the Brazilian Amazon : a sense of
space / Janet M. Chernela. — 1st ed.
        p.   cm.
    Includes bibliographical references and index.
    ISBN 0-292-78522-4 (alk. paper)
    1. Guanano Indians.   2. Social status—Case studies.   I. Title.
F2520.1.G72C47   1993
981'.13—dc20   92-4734

In memory of
Hannah Seidman Moss
and
Robert F. Murphy

Contents

Illustrations

Figures

Tables

Preface

THIS WORK IS A CASE STUDY of the Wanano, a group defined by a distinct language, name, and ancestral history. I was initially drawn to the region of the Uaupés River basin in the Northwest Amazon by reading Irving Goldman's 1939 ethnography of the Cubeo, neighbors and in-laws of the Wanano.[1] Good ethnographies raise thoughtful questions and Goldman's raised many. Among them was the character of a social ranking system not found elsewhere in Amazonia, a phenomenon unexplained in the literature on the region.

Like other Eastern Tukanoan–speaking peoples of the area, the Wanano think of themselves as a single descent group organized through common putative ancestry. The Wanano are internally subdivided into localized descent groups, known to ethnologists as patri-clans or sibs. A sense of siblingship unites members of the language group at every level. An emphasis on seniority, on the other hand, differentiates them: every individual within a sib, and every sib within a language group, stands in a fixed rank relation to every other. The order of seniority is reproduced through the inheritance of names in each succeeding generation. Rank, a scalar, sequential ordering of seniority, governs the interrelationships of subgroups within the whole.

My interest in the phenomenon of ranking was heightened by an incident that occurred early in my fieldwork. On arriving at the Wanano village of Wapu in 1978, I began to elicit terms of address in order to make sense of the relations among the 160 people in the village.[2] I assumed that the terms themselves, such as "my father," would be neutral and public, even as they provided a key to the familial relationships of the members of the village. I had imagined this to be a sensible course and that my inquiry would be regarded as courteous and nonintrusive.

In many small-scale societies people are addressed by kinship terms, and this is true for the Wanano. The terms are ordinarily reciprocal: for example, if you call someone "my father," he will call you "my child," and so on. A survey of such terms should produce a symmetrical grid showing complementary pairs of terms for referent and referee or addresser and addressee.

My survey proved revealing, but not for the reasons I had supposed. One entire household was out of kilter with the rest of the village. Each member of this family reported calling everyone else a "younger" relative, which meant that the others should return the address by calling them "older." Instead, the other villagers claimed to call them "younger."

When I began listening to village conversations, however, I found that the unusual family was reporting one thing and doing another. Furthermore, there was a pattern to the discrepancy. In fact, all members of this family were called "younger" by all other villagers and returned the reply with kin terms preceded by "older." But why conceal something so seemingly innocuous as form of address?

I soon learned that address is the form of speech that carries information regarding status position. Individuals in a Wanano village are ranked, with no two individuals occupying the same position. In any dyad, one person is always the senior and the other the junior, indicated in speech by metaphors of relative age. These status positions are based upon inheritance from father to offspring. While thinking that I was making an innocent inquiry, I had unwittingly placed one family in a somewhat humiliating position. I later learned they were from a lower-ranked sib than the other villagers.[3]

My investigation into terms of address eventually led me to discover that the low-ranked sib was in dispute with the other, more highly ranked villagers. Indeed, I later came to understand that the village was wrenched apart by factions and witchcraft accusations, reflective of and expressed through tensions related to rank.

Because I resided with a leading family of one of those factions, I was perceived to be allied with it. Once this became clear to me, I removed myself from Wapu to the refuge of nearby Yapima, the Wanano village where I established bonds of meaningful friendship and the feeling of being at home. My experience during those earliest days in Wapu, nevertheless, served to call my attention to the relevance of the dispute I had witnessed.

The discordances demonstrated by the family from Wapu are indicative not merely of personal emotions, though these are sincerely felt. On another level, they are representations of tensions that are inherent in the society itself. As such, they point to the fracture zones of a social system.

Anthropologists justifiably focus on agreed-upon systems of meaning. Rank is one such system. Yet divergence from standards is of equal importance to our understanding of society. The dissenting position of a sib at odds with higher-ranked villagers, presented in private to an outsider, suggests deeper, albeit covert, dissonance and opposition to an apparently coherent and unified social order.

The emphasis on rank at Wapu and the passions it generated continued to intrigue me. Other Amazonian populations had no such social forms. Rank appeared to be a central principle governing social relations of kin groups and individuals among the Wanano, as well as a locus of contested identities; thus, my initial interest in rank was affirmed and I continued to make it the focus of my inquiry.

This book discusses rank as a major principle that, with intermarriage, organizes the social and economic life of the Wanano. The introduction orients the reader to the Wanano and to the major theoretical issues addressed in the book. In it I briefly outline two theoretical models that attempt to explain ranked society, then review the research of other Uaupés specialists and suggest how my study differs from and complements theirs. The distribution of rank structures and their relative importance in the upriver (Colombian) and downriver (Brazilian) sections of the Uaupés suggests, I believe, fundamental principles and features of rank systems in general.

Chapter 2 places the social system in a historic context of population movements, warfare, and encroaching European expansion, considering the relationship of political consolidation and marriage practice to warfare. This chapter locates politics not in the descent group, but in a different sphere: marriage. Here I argue that the unusual prevailing practice of linguistic exogamy in the Northwest Amazon can best be explained through an analysis of historic factors. I rely upon Wanano oral histories to demonstrate the role of obligatory language group exogamy for alliance formation in a context of neighboring predatory chiefdoms.

Chapter 3 reviews the activities of scientific travelers, missionaries, and state agencies in the Uaupés basin from 1760 to the present. The impact of European expansion upon Uaupés culture is considered in greater detail.

Chapters 4 and 5 are concerned with social organization and kinship, respectively. They describe in depth the two organizing principles of Uaupés social organization—rank, a system of internal subdivisions within exogamous, linguistically distinct patrilineal descent groups; and linguistic exogamy, with its countervailing matrices of social linkages that connect different language groups to each other.

Chapter 6 presents Wanano notions of "placement" and "displacement" and the sentiments attached to them as portrayed in spontaneously composed songs. This chapter conveys the experience of living in such a system, especially as it affects in-marrying women.

Chapter 7 takes up production, emphasizing the commensurability of abundance in the physical environment with the manifestation of "succulence," which indicates social seniority. Here social production and the production of the social are inseparable. This point is further explored in chapter 8, where the exchange system shows the requirements of seniors to give abundantly.

Chapters 9 and 10 reveal the dynamic processes that underlie an apparently static system. Chapter 9 relates the concepts of seniority, production, and exchange by examining the dramatic confrontation between an ineffective chief and villagers who attempt a work stoppage. In chapter 10 a low-ranking sib claims the site and status of a dying senior sib; its one remaining member is forced into an exile which she describes in a song she composes in flight. Here rank is shown to be a social product subject to negotiation and maneuver.

In foregrounding processes of change, these last chapters return the book to the issues of history and structure addressed at the opening. "Contradictions are vital agencies of change and are central to historic processes in all societies. . . . Indeed, the tension . . . may be the structure and not a sign of its demise" (Murphy 1986: 42). The insight sheds light on the "unrepresentable" events of history and their role in the construction and reconstruction of society. It also sheds light on the family at Wapu and its attempts to negotiate an ostensibly nonnegotiable social fact.

At a time when anthropology has become increasingly fragmented and specialized, this work is an attempt to return to the traditions of a comprehensive anthropology envisioned by Franz Boas—one that considers within its scope the full spectrum of social life. At the same time, the work attempts to utilize the specialized lexicons and discourse styles that have emerged from a number of subdisciplines. My attempt at multivocality is in response to the idea exemplified by the parable of the blind men describing an elephant: a multiplicity of perspectives is expected to yield greater insight than would any single viewpoint. In order to soften the contrast of discourse styles, I have divided the book into four parts entitled History, Sociology, Ecology and Economy, and Ordinary Dramas. A concluding discussion reworks the material and languages of the book into a summarizing, integrated statement.

Acknowledgments

THE PROCESS OF CREATING A BOOK begins long before the actual writing. My choice to study in the Northwest Amazon was inspired by the excellent ethnographies of Irving Goldman and Gerardo Reichel-Dolmatoff (no other monographs existed at the time), and the articles of Kaj Århem, Christine and Stephen Hugh-Jones, Jean Jackson, Pierre-Yves Jacopin, and Arthur Sorensen. At the time I worked as an assistant to Robert Carneiro, curator of South American ethnology at the American Museum of Natural History. He alerted me to the literature on the region and to some of the prominent questions relating to it. I spoke with Jean Jackson and Gertrude Dole before going to the field and was aided by their encouragement and advice. Preparations for the field were particularly eased by the experienced counsel of friends Sheila Dauer, Anne Farber, Stephanie Fins, Carol Kramer, Louise Lennihan, Yolanda Murphy, and Glenn Petersen.

In Brazil, I was given friendship and guidance by numerous people, particularly Roberto Cardoso de Oliveira, Roque Laraia, Alcida Ramos, Berta Ribeiro, Ana Gita de Oliveira, Anthony Seeger, and Peter Silverwood-Cope. On my first trip into the upper Rio Negro in 1978, I was accompanied by Berta Ribeiro, whose companionship I found invaluable and whose friendship I continue to cherish.

The Wanano villages are located on the Uaupés River a distance of 60 km or five days' travel by canoe from the Salesian Mission and airstrip at Iauareté. In 1978 access required the authorization of FUNAI (the National Indian Foundation) and approval by the Brazilian Air Force (FAB), which alone flew into the region. I wish to thank these two agencies and the many officials who provided these permissions. Flights into the region were irregular, with many stopovers. A frequent overnight stop was São Gabriel da Cachoeira, where I was warmly and generously received by the family of Pedro and Miriam Zani. Before and after each four- to six-month stay in the Wanano villages, the Salesian Mission of Iauaretê provided me with hospitality. Among the administrators of the Iauaretê Mission, I wish to thank Irmã Anunciata, then director of the mission school, and Irmã Alina, the outstanding physician at the school. Furthermore, I wish to acknowledge my gratitude to Padre Antonio Scolaro, who, before his untimely death, was the conscientious director of the Mission at Iauaretê; Padre Victor Lobo, who replaced him; and Padre Miguel Scott. When, on one occasion, I was bitten by jungle dogs and unable to walk, the artifact collector Richard Melnyk went out of his way to help in every manner.

I would also like to thank Nathan and Carolyn Waltz of the Summer (Wycliffe) Institute of Linguistics, who shared with me their knowledge of the Colombian Wanano. Their important linguistic studies were of great assistance to me in learning the language. I also wish to thank the pilot Jim Yost and his family for their extraordinary moral and tactical support.

In 1980, following the first phase of field research, I joined the faculty of the Brazilian Institute for Amazonian Research (Instituto Nacional de Pesquisas da Amazônia or INPA) in Manaus. I am particularly grateful for the support given me by the former directors of INPA, Drs. Warwick Estevam Kerr, Eneas Salati, Henrique Bergamin Filho, Herbert Schubart, and M. de Nazaré Góes Ribeiro. I was fortunate to be at INPA during a period of remarkable intellectual activity and comradeship. Among numerous friends and colleagues, I wish to mention Rob Bierregaard, Philip Fearnside, Michael Goulding, Bill Magnussen, Jorge Nakamura, Adelia de Oliveira (of Conselho Nacional de Desenvolvimento Científico e Tecnológico or CNPq), David Oren, Judy Rankin, Lisa and Nigel Smith, Kelly St. John, and Ilse Walker and to make special mention of those with whom I have carried out collaborative work: Jorge Arias, Vernon Thatcher, and Evaldete Ferraz de Oliveira.

I am also indebted to Naercio Menezes of the Museu de Zoologia de São Paulo and to Richard Vari and Stanley Weitzman of the Smithsonian for their assistance in fish identification; as well as to William Rodrigues of the Departamento de Botânica at INPA for help in identifying plant specimens. I would like to make special mention of the invaluable assistance I received from João-Bosco Marinho and Crispiniano Carvalho, who helped collect specimens and data, and from Sherre Nelson and Megumi Yamakoshi, who helped process these collections.

An early version of this manuscript was presented as a doctoral dissertation in the Department of Anthropology of Columbia University. In that endeavor, I received valuable encouragement and advice from Drs. Robert F. Murphy, Robert Carneiro, Gertrude Dole, Irving Goldman, Morton Fried, and Alexander Alland. Joy Travalino assisted me in processing numerical data and Jill Bauer in German translation. Joanne Roy prepared the illustrations. Of the many people who offered me friendship and support, I would like to mention Brian Burkhalter, Renate Clynes, Shirley Chernela, Bruce Cohen, Hilda Frank, Susan Golla, Jonathan Hill, Harriet Klein, Rima Shore, Laila Willemsen, Robin Wright, Timothy Yuan, and Ted Zent.

The transition from doctoral dissertation into book would not have been possible without the assistance of David Maybury-Lewis, who generously provided me with an office in which to prepare the manuscript and the opportunity to utilize the extensive anthropology collections of the Tozzer Library in the Peabody Museum of Harvard University. I am grateful to him, as I am to other members of Cultural Survival (including Ted Macdonald, Jason Clay, and Pia Maybury-Lewis), for the good company and atmosphere of dedication in which the manuscript was written.

In addition, I am grateful for the important sources of support provided me by Florida International University, where I am a faculty member. April and Ken Buscher, Peter Craumer, Hugh Gladwin, James Mau, Lisandro Perez, Joyce Petersen, and Mark Rosenberg are among those who contributed time and resources so that this work might be completed. The book and the author owe much to my close friend and colleague Eric Leed for his insightful reading of the manuscript.

It has been my privilege to work with three eminent mentors: Robert Carneiro, Irving Goldman, and Robert Murphy. It was Robert Carneiro who introduced me to the issues of South American ethnology and to the practice of anthropology when I worked as his assistant at the American Museum of Natural History. He has continued to be both an example and a principal source of support, stimulation, and friendship. I wish, too, to express special gratitude to Irving Goldman, the "senior" of northwest Amazon research, whose classic monograph *The Cubeo* inspired my own research. His enthusiastic encouragement over the years has been essential to my own maturation as a student of Tukanoan society.

Most profound gratitude must go to Robert F. Murphy, under whose study I initiated this project twelve years before his death in 1990. Murphy was ill during many of the years during which I worked with him, yet his energies and dogged determination remained surprisingly unflagging. Indeed, Murphy's keen intellect and insight into humanity were deepened by his confrontation with his own mortality. His forbearance and standards of excellence and creativity have been, and continue to be, a source of inspiration.

A number of people whose support has been indirect, though no less essential, deserve mention. They are Heidi, Stephanie, and Richard Von Schmertzing, Verna Gillis, and Stephen Mount.

Greatest tribute and appreciation is owed to the Wanano and in-marrying wives of other language groups. The student of the Northwest Amazon is fortunate, for the Eastern Tukanoans, such as the Wanano, are proud of their heritage and are excellent teachers. I am able to thank only a fraction of the people to whom I am indebted. By registered name, they are Ricardo Teixeira, Carmen Almeida, Vitorina Chaves, José Cordeiro, Nicho Marquez, Paulo Marquez, Pedro Melo, Candido Melo, Manuel Teixeira, Celina Teixeira, Iginu Teixeira, Armando Trinidade, and Emilia Trinidade. Nicho Marquez asked that her words be heard "in the big city." This book, in a way, is hers.

Funding for this study was provided by the Social Science Research Council, the Fulbright-Hays program of the U.S. Department of Education, the Instituto Nacional de Pesquisas da Amazônia (INPA), the Florida Endowment for Higher Education, and the Advanced Research section of the Social Science Research Council (Joint Committee on Latin American Studies of the American Council with funds provided by the National Endowment for the Humanities, the Ford Foundation, and the Andrew W. Mellon Foundation).

Notes on the Transcription

IN TRANSCRIBING WANANO COMMON NOUNS, I use the letter k to indicate a velar stop (the k sound in the English word "key"). The same sound is represented in written Portuguese, Spanish, and *língua geral* by the letters *c* or *q*, as in the Portuguese and Spanish *tocar* and *toque* (or the *língua geral, aracú,* and Querarí). I use the letter k to portray this sound so that I may follow it with an *h* to indicate an aspiration. I reserve *ch* for the palatalized, voiceless alveolar affricate, in common Wanano usage. This sound is represented in Spanish and English by the same orthography, as shown in the Spanish *coche* and the English "chilly." The same *ch* sound may also be accurately illustrated by the symbol *č*, although this orthographic form is less widely recognized than *ch*.

Where proper nouns, such as place names, have a written precedent, I follow the established forms. This is the case even when Wanano place names have conventional spellings, such as the village names Bucacopa and Carurú. In Amazonia, many tribal and place names are by convention in *língua geral*, a derivative of indigenous Tupi-Guaraní. Therefore, while Wanano transcriptions employ the letter k for an unaspirated voiceless velar stop, proper nouns with written precedents may use *c* for the same sound (Carurú, not Karurú). For a more comprehensive treatment of Wanano, see Waltz (1976).

The following is a key to pronouncing some of the orthographic symbols used in this text:

Transcription Key

k unaspirated voiceless velar stop
kh aspirated voiceless velar stop
x voiceless velar spirant (like the Spanish *j*)

ü   high front rounded vowel (as in French *sûr*)

ch   palatalized voiceless aveolar affricate

ʔ   voiceless glottal stop

h   voiceless fricative

THE WANANO INDIANS OF THE BRAZILIAN AMAZON

Chapter 1. Introduction

A TUKANOAN COMPANION AND I going to Rio de Janeiro once made a tourist stop at the summer palace of Brazil's first imperial family.[1] The palace was full of the sumptuous display of nineteenth-century royalty, including a throne room. The room was dominated by the imposing presence of the throne—an ornately decorated chair located on a raised platform. My Tukanoan companion turned to me and asked, "Does the emperor kneel before his people or do the people kneel before the emperor?"

For the Wanano and other Eastern Tukanoans who are without figures of comparable authority, there is no assumption that a leader is inherently powerful. My companion's question places the locus of power not in a leader per se, but in a relationship. For this reason, knowing the implications of the kneeling gesture, she wonders which is the more appropriate: who does kneel before whom?

This work is a case study of the Wanano, a Native American society in the Northwest Amazon, unusual in Amazonia in having rigidly bounded descent groups and ascribed social statuses. These amount to, in Wanano terms, vertical and horizontal "placements." The book takes this system of placement or rank as its focus.

Ranked systems, defining status difference, but lacking political centers, are found throughout the world, yet we know surprisingly little about them. Our models for civil society neglect this form, proceeding as they do from models of state development in which centralized political power is seen as essential in the structuring of rank. This is not so in the case of the northwest Amazon.

The Wanano in Uaupés Society

Approximately 1,500 speakers of Wanano, a language of the Eastern Tukanoan family, inhabit the middle Uaupés[2] basin in Colombia and Brazil.[3] The Wanano constitute one unit in a larger intermarrying population of twenty or more language groups who occupy the Uaupés and other headwater streams of the Rio Negro, a region known in the literature as the Northwest Amazon.

For the Wanano and linguistically related populations, language is considered a manifestation of descent, with speakers of the same language thought to be members of one patrilineal descent group within which marriage is prohibited.[4]

As a result of the widespread practice of linguistic exogamy, approximately 14,000 speakers of diverse and sometimes distant language groups, inhabiting some 150,000 km[2] in adjacent areas of Colombia, Venezuela, and Brazil, are related either by kin or in-law ties. The result is a uniquely coherent culture complex, which has patrilineal descent and cross-cousin marriage as major integrating structural principles.

On the basis of established literary convention (Jackson 1974, 1983) and the Wanano emphasis on language as the primary feature of personal and group identity, I refer to the Wanano as a "language group," a shorthand for the more precise, but longer, "linguistic-descent group."[5]

Researchers (Jackson 1974; Sorensen 1967) have called attention to the remarkable degree of multilingualism and language group exogamy in the Northwest Amazon. The linguist Arthur Sorensen (1967) presents us with a useful classification of Eastern Tukanoan languages, identifying thirteen languages as members of the Eastern Tukanoan language family: Tukano, Tuyuka, Yurutí, Paneroa, Eduria, Carapana, Tatuyo, Barasana, Piratapuya, Wanano, Desana, Siriano, and Cubeo.[6] Sorensen suggests that the Eastern Tukanoan languages are less closely related to each other than are languages of the Romance group.

Sorensen estimates at 10,000 the population of speakers of Eastern Tukanoan languages. The total intermarrying population of the Northwest Amazon increases to approximately 14,000 when non-Tukanoan speakers are considered.[7] The cluster of Eastern Tukanoan societies is bounded on the north, south, and northeast by Arawakan speakers and to the west by Cariban speakers. These neighboring groups enter the Eastern Tukanoan system of extratribal marriage. Two Arawakan-speaking groups, the Tariana and the Baniwa, have intermarried with the Wanano over generations.[8]

The Wanano regard four other language groups as agnatic kin and extend marriage prohibitions to them: the Piratapuya, Arapaço, Siriano, and Tuyuka (see fig. 1). Theoretically all other groups are marriageable, but some lack the established alliances that would make them ongoing in-laws. From the perspective of the Wanano

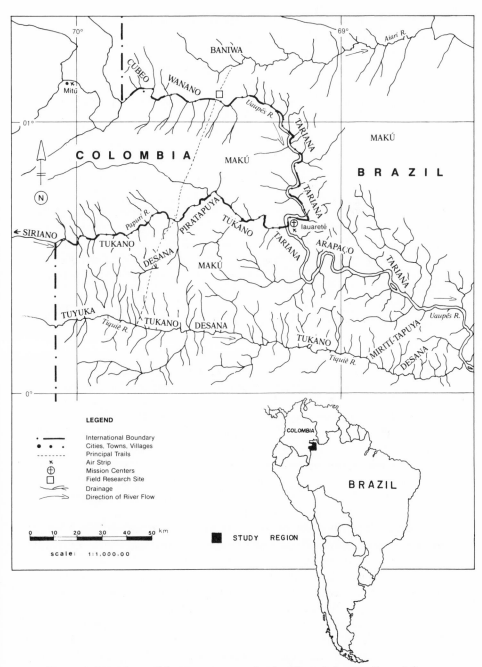

Figure 1. Locations of language groups in the Uaupés basin. Copyright 1992 by Janet M. Chernela.

and all other members of their multilanguage phratry, the world in this way divides into two complementary units: "brothers" and "marriageables."

Wanano both maintain ongoing affinity with other language groups over generations and forge new marriage alliances where ongoing affinity has not been established. In such a system new populations are easily accommodated as in-laws.

The Wanano

The Wanano call themselves Kotiria and are called Okotikana by the Tukano, Okodyiwa by the Cubeo, and Panumapa by the Tariana. The group, however, is most commonly known in Brazil as the Uanano or Uanana and in Colombia as the Guanano or Guanana; this naming follows the historic convention of translating the native name into *língua geral.* The spelling "Wanano" is perhaps the clearest transcription of the *língua geral* pronunciation and the one most consistent with established international norms.[9]

Brazil's ten Wanano settlements are situated 3 to 24 km apart along a continuous stretch of the middle course of the main river.[10] Each settlement contains from 30 to 160 persons; I estimate the total Wanano population in Brazil to number about 500 to 600. When we add the approximately 180 Wanano who live on the southern, Colombian bank of the Uaupés and the 800 Wanano cited by Nathan Waltz (1976: iii) as living in the Colombian Vaupés Territory, the Wanano population totals some 1,500 to 1,600 individuals.[11]

Villages consist of mud or bark houses with thatch roofs located on high ground along the river edge. Houses are situated in a rectangle around a common plaza parallel to, and in view of, the river. Paths lead from a canoe landing to the residential area. Each house has a front entry onto the plaza and a rear door that opens onto paths that proceed through the surrounding forest to gardens and streams.

Wanano subsist largely on root-crop cultivation and fishing. Fish provides the principal source of protein, and manioc the principal source of carbohydrates. These items, and the utensils used to gather or process them, are essential to the sharing of resources, which occurs informally within a settlement on a daily basis and more intermittently and formally among different local settlements. Minimal exploitation of resources characterizes day-to-day life; intensive exploitation occurs prior to the occasional elaborate exchange ceremonies described in later chapters.

The Uaupés River at the center of Wanano life is a black headwater stream of the Rio Negro, a principal tributary of the Amazon.

The Uaupés rises in the rainforests of eastern Colombia and follows a southeastward course through the villages of the Wanano into Brazil, where it enters the Rio Negro near São Gabriel da Cachoeira.

Although it drains a section of neotropical rainforest noted for its especially high rainfall, the forest cover here is sparse, relative to rainforests elsewhere. The impoverished soils through which the Uaupés flows give rise to forests and rivers of low nutrient content and relatedly low plant and animal life. Against this depauperate backdrop, the richness of cultural life stands in sharp contrast.

Descent Group Organization

The social organizations of the Wanano and other Indians inhabiting Brazil's Uaupés River basin differ from those of other Amazonian societies in that they are internally ordered into a series of scaled, named subunits proceeding from most senior, or first, to least senior, or last.

An origin myth shared by Eastern Tukanoan speakers tells of a sacred anaconda-canoe that journeys upriver from a primordial Water Door and swims underwater to the region of the Uaupés River. Reaching the headwaters, the anaconda-canoe turns around so that its head faces downriver and its tail upriver. It then slowly rises, and from the segmentations of its body emerge the first ancestors of each of the patrilineal kin groups of the Uaupés. Those who emerge from the head of the anaconda are designated as seniors, the "heads" of the local patrilineal descent groups or sibs.[12] Analogously, sibs that emerge upriver are known as "tails."

The anaconda of the Northwest Amazon differs from other serpentine motifs, such as the ouroboros portrayed in Mediterranean iconography as a snake with its tail in its mouth, precisely in the directionality of the Amazonian usage. Positioning is crucial, for the birth order of sibs from the body of the ancestor becomes an order of status fixing the relations between distinct subsections of language groups.

The anaconda *qua* river, then, is an image that is used to represent the creation of a sociotopographical order and the emplacement of peoples. As a primary metonymy, the river may be said to be a birth canal, a "corridor" of ancestors, a boundary that separates differences and connects them. It is also a source of sustenance and social distinction.

Although deep genealogies are absent, the language group is conceptualized by its members as a group of agnates who trace descent from a set of ancestral founding brothers who emerged from the primordial anaconda canoe. Each of the twenty-five Wanano sib subdivisions recognizes one of the founding siblings as its focal ancestor. As the ancestral siblings are ranked according to seniority specified in the origin traditions of each sib, the entire language group is united in a comprehensive hierarchy.

Social distinctions within the Wanano language group are maintained and reproduced through a naming system in which each Wanano sib owns a set of exclusive ancestral names. The operative rule is that first-born is senior to second-born, and so on down the line; and that the descendants of first-born ancestors are senior to descendants of later-born ancestors. The basis of the terminology is thus inherited seniority, rather than actual age. Rank, then, is a language of social positioning, a linguistic and conceptual placement of individuals and groups in relation to one another.

Rank is manifest on a daily basis in the terms of relative address used by speakers in conversation and greeting. Also, rank statuses are associated with roles and expectations that are especially foregrounded in ritual. High-ranked groups are said to be "succulent" and are expected to manifest this trait through generous display in the sponsorship of large dance ceremonies. Such "succulence" is thought to be an attribute both inherent in status and a product of it.

Descendants of the first of the twenty-five ancestral brothers are called "our eldest brothers" and are known as "chiefs." As descendants of the youngest ancestral brothers are the lowest in rank and are referred to as "younger brothers," "the lasts," or "servers,"[13] so the highest-ranked sibs are seen as "donors."

Although ranking produces a hierarchy of individuals, titles, and influence, it entails neither differences in wealth nor coercive controls of labor. Relatedly, the terms "server" and "servant," universally employed in the literature on the northwest Amazon, reference identities and roles that point to service as their prominent feature. Yet these must be understood in the very specific terms of Eastern Tukanoan society. Wealth is never accumulated by individuals or groups, nor service controlled. As a result of practices and values that generate reciprocity at every level of the social order, the ultimate outcome of representational ranking is substantive equality.

The Concept of the Ranked Society

The phenomenon of ranking in societies lacking both political centers and resource accumulation has been of theoretical interest to students of political and social systems for some time.

The concept of the ranked society emerges from centuries of scholarship on the nature of social inequality. Enlightenment scholars refuted the Aristotelian notion of inequality as an inherent, natural phenomenon, advancing in its place a two-stage model of social development, in which an egalitarian phase precedes stratification. Rousseau, Marx, and others believed that the introduction of private property spurs this transformation.

The traditional two-stage model does not account for the many societies reported by anthropologists that are neither egalitarian nor stratified. Although an extensive literature documents these societies (e.g., Sahlins 1958; Goldman 1957; Malinowski 1922; Leach 1954), we do not yet have a body of ethnographic data adequate to shed light on how such societies function or to provide a basis for comparative analysis. Furthermore, the scant available data derive primarily from island societies; few continental ranked societies have been documented.

The social organizations of the Indians inhabiting Brazil's Uaupés River basin, then, represent an exceptional case in the literature of a present-day ranked society inhabiting the continental tropical lowlands.

The operation of such ranked societies appears to be anomalous: by fixating degrees of prestige and identifying positions of authority, rank subverts egalitarianism. Yet, while a ranking system realizes an ideology of fixed statuses and levels, groups and individuals have little actual power and no military capacity to support their positions; it allows for maneuverability. In this sense, rank does not necessarily imply a strictly nonegalitarian, stratified society. Ranked societies, in short, defy categorization as egalitarian or nonegalitarian, for they are at once both and neither.

The anthropological literature contains extensive commentary on the distinctive criteria of ranked society and the roots of its development. One school holds that the economic factor—the redistribution of production—is critical; another stresses the political factor—the supralocal organization or chiefdom that results from warfare. As this work shows, these two major approaches may be complementary rather than contradictory.

In this study I take a different tack, by arguing that the unique feature characterizing ranked societies is a particular type of organization of work not found in egalitarian societies. This position encompasses both political and economic factors. Moreover, the study places the politics of warfare not in the realm of descent group organization but elsewhere: in marriage.

This book addresses not the origins of the rank level of society, but rather its dynamics. It emphasizes the key element of production and demonstrates the embeddedness of rank in contexts that are simultaneously political, economic, and ideological.

In *Argonauts of the Western Pacific* (1922) Bronislaw Malinowski speaks of rank as a form of social differentiation among the Trobriand Islanders and uses the "insignia of rank and authority" (1922: 52) as a basis for distinguishing them from other Melanesian societies.

Morton Fried uses "rank societies" to distinguish a discrete category of political organization—a level of complexity different from either stratified or egalitarian society. His definition is useful: "The rank society is characterized by having fewer positions of valued status than individuals capable of handling them. Furthermore, most rank societies have a fixed number of such positions, neither expanding them nor diminishing them with fluctuations in the population, save as totally new segmented units originate . . . or disappear . . ." (1960: 717).

In Sahlins' (1958) typology of stratification based upon degree, he speaks of "ranking systems" (1958: 2) to describe various types of stratification. In the same work, Sahlins identifies redistribution as the basis of chiefdoms and posits the adaptability of hierarchy in the equitable distribution of resources. His early positions have formed the basis for a continuing debate on the issue of rank.

Elman Service (1962) follows Sahlins in focusing on redistributive aspects of ranked societies. Using the term "chiefdom" to designate a society both denser than a tribe and organized through coordinating centers of economic, social, and religious activities, Service attributes the rise of chiefdoms to "a total environmental situation which was selective for specialization in production and redistribution of produce from a controlling center. The resulting organic basis of social integration made possible a more integrated society, and the increased efficiency in production and distribution made possible a denser society" (1962: 133–134).

Distinguishing political from economic factors, Fried faults Service for confusing the product of ranking (i.e., redistribution) with its cause. For Fried, the regularity of the redistributive role "conveys prestige and bolsters political status" (1967: 118). For him, "Rank has no necessary connection to economic status in any of its forms, though it does acquire economic significance. The point is that rank can and in some instances does exist totally independent of the economic order" (1967: 52).

Fried does not minimize the importance of redistribution to rank systems, but emphasizes intrasocietal conflict rather than integration as the more powerful explanation. While Fried, Sahlins, and Service all stress the key role of a redistribution center in ranked society, the three differ on how economic factors create, or reflect, the power structure.

Anthropologists have not unanimously viewed redistribution as the salient feature organizing ranked societies. Timothy Earle (1977), Christopher Peebles and Susan Kus (1977), and Robert Carneiro (1981, 1991) question this emphasis. Carneiro departs from the views of Sahlins and Service in the following way: "Service appears to have been strongly influenced by Sahlins' work on Polynesia, and like him, saw chiefdoms as having an economic rather than political basis. . . . Like Sahlins, Service saw chiefdoms as essentially economic in origin and function. He failed to perceive their basically political nature" (1981: 43).

Carneiro rejects the category "rank" and refers to chiefdoms,[14] since in his view a more crucial factor is a level of political organization in which numerous local communities can be amalgamated under a single leader. He believes that hierarchy emerges in response to warfare, particularly warfare that results from population density and consequent circumscription (Carneiro 1970, 1987).[15] Warfare in this way becomes the only mechanism that has the power to transcend the political autonomy of settlements.

Carneiro defines a chiefdom as "an autonomous political unit comprising a number of communities under the permanent control of a paramount chief" (1991: 168). By such reckoning, the Wanano would be intermediate between an egalitarian system and a chiefdom since they show more status differentiation than egalitarian societies but less political consolidation than chiefdoms. Societies such as this are neither fish nor fowl for they are not chiefdoms, but neither are they egalitarian bands or tribes.

Review of Rank in the Literature on the Uaupés Region

When the data reported in this study are compared to other research from the Uaupés area, a number of important patterns emerge. First, my data stress rank and horizontal linkages that cross-cut descent, whereas earlier works on the Uaupés, based upon Colombian cases, have emphasized segmentary descent and egalitarian principles. For example, Jean Jackson's rich ethnographic work on the Bará of the upper Colombian Uaupés (1972, 1983) devotes relatively little attention to rank. It appears, however, that many features of rank described for Colombian, upriver groups correspond to ranking among the Wanano. Jackson reports, for example, that a sib's rank is based upon a model of birth order and that lower-ranked sibs are considered to be recent: "Another way to indicate a sib's low rank is to say during a recital of the sib's origin myth that the sib's ancestor did not in fact come from . . . 'breast-milk river' . . . but was picked up later . . ." (1972: 68). Jackson finds, moreover, that "at times the low-ranking sibs of a given Tukanoan group will be described as being servants to the higher-ranking sibs—hunting for game and carrying out other tasks in a manner parallel to Makú activities" (Jackson 1983: 152). Bará informants state that low-ranking sibs were at one time savage, ("Makú-like"), and that they speak "ungrammatically" (1972: 67, 68).

For the Bará, seniority is a feature of terminology only in sibling terms (Jackson 1972, 1977, 1983). In this way the Bará differ from the Wanano and other Uaupés groups. Jackson mentions that among the neighboring Tuyuka, with a greater number of sibs, "a person [shows] . . . that he is of a much higher ranked sib than the person he is addressing by calling that person grandfather and being called grandchild" (1976: 68).

Jackson nevertheless describes Uaupés society as "egalitarian," without "a significant amount of exclusive control of scarce resources by different social units" (1976: 68; 1983: 212). She also states that "no discernible social units occupy distinct economic niches or locate their settlements at particular strategic points in the landscape" (1976: 68). In the same article, she mentions "well-established rules of hospitality," but remarks that "excessive demands are rarely made on the hosts" (1976: 69). New data suggest that these are characteristic distinctions between upriver and downriver groups.

Two exceptions to the generalization that Uaupés societies are egalitarian are recent studies by Irving Goldman and Christine Hugh-Jones. Together with my own work, these exceptions suggest an explanation for the apparently different emphases the Bará and Wanano place on rank.

Irving Goldman's early ethnography, *The Cubeo* (1963), was based upon fieldwork carried out in 1939 among a low-ranking Cubeo sib called the Bahukiwa. This ethnography, the first in-depth account of a Northwest Amazon society, describes the distinctive Cubeo culture, while identifying elements shared with the larger cultural complex of the Northwest Amazon.

In 1981 Goldman revisited the Cubeo to work among high-ranked groups. Goldman's later analysis of the Cubeo (1981), based on this fieldwork, lays greater stress on rank than did his previous reports.

These findings resulted in several publications on the key symbols and metaphors of Cubeo hierarchy.

In Goldman's later work he discusses the symbolic bases of "the linear order of hierarchy," conceived of by the Cubeo as "an organic and spatial concept pertaining to the body of the anaconda and the structure of the river" (1981: 10). He draws attention to the grandparent-grandchild dyad: "In this dyad there is reciprocity: the nurturing grandparents gain their personal immortality by giving their names, their specific spiritual attributes, to their grandchildren. They live again through them. But since these are also chiefs and servants to each other . . . [it] is clearly ambivalent in its intimations for social status" (1981: 16). "Chiefs and servants are bound within the special metaphysical dyad of grandchild/grandparent with its functions of nurtured and nurturer" (1981: 21). Goldman's description of these complementary relationships is derived from informant "recollection" of a former period, when chiefly groups reportedly were a leisure class that neither cultivated nor foraged, tended to by their servants. Goldman suspects, as I do, that this description is distorted and "imbue[d] . . . with some of the qualities of present relations with Colombian *patrones*" (1981: 21).

Goldman now characterizes the Uaupés system as an "elementary hereditary aristocracy" (1981: 1). His study reveals the symbolic analogies underlying the relationship of chief to servant, or grandchild to grandparent, as it obtained in an earlier, hypothesized period. Both of these reconstructions provide strong evidence for horizontal structures in the Colombian Uaupés, comparable, though not identical, to organizations I was able to observe in the Brazilian Uaupés.

The analyses of Stephen and Christine Hugh-Jones, based upon fieldwork among the Barasana of the Pirá-Paraná River in Colombia between 1968 and 1969, form a unit that integrates myth, ritual, and everyday reality of the Northwest Amazon.[16] Christine Hugh-Jones (1979) posits a hierarchically organized system of five interdependent sibs, each having a specialized role. Of the five specialized roles—chief, dancer/chanter, warrior, shaman, and servant—she reports that only the dancer/chanter and shaman remain well defined; the chief, warrior, and servant roles having been lost with time. She locates all five roles in a symmetrical model of three domains: the politico-economic, the metaphysical, and the externally oriented domain.

In this model of five functionally interdependent, specialized sibs, Hugh-Jones finds sibs associated with two of these roles (shaman and chanter) and postulates the "missing roles of chiefs, warriors, and servants" (1979: 54) on the basis of informants' recollections. The Wanano provide evidence for the existence of sibs in the "chief" and "servant" categories, but suggest a pattern of localized interdependent pairs as opposed to local complements of five.

What accounts for the variation in different reports? Does it suggest patterning? To what variables can we link "more rank" and "less rank," and what does this reveal with regard to rank structures in general? The Wanano case, in its complexity, provides a fruitful setting for approaching these questions.

A number of significant patterns differentiate upriver and downriver groups. The most apparent is size. Christine Hugh-Jones gives population figures for thirteen upriver settlements, which range from four persons to twenty-nine persons (1979: 42); the average community size is fourteen. Irving Goldman (1963: 25) reports twenty-nine residence sites for the Cuduiarí, "each averaging some 30 to 35 people." Jean Jackson (1976: 68) describes nucleated villages of "one to four small houses" separated from one another by two to ten hours of canoe travel. In the longhouse settlements of the upper Papurí, the area in which she worked, she describes "fewer than thirty individuals" (1976: 73) per settlement.

In contrast, downriver sites are large. The largest Wanano settlement held 160 persons between 1978 and 1981 and was located less than an hour's walking distance from a village of 82 persons. Koch-Grünberg (1909) reported a population of 200 for the same settlement in 1902. The population of the settlement in which I was based was 77. In short, the average size of downriver settlements is three to four times the size of upriver settlements.

Resource availability is another factor distinguishing upriver and downriver settlements. Downriver locations are the more strategic in terms of environmental and technologically related factors. Due to the dendritic pattern of rivers, river size and fish supply are related. With each bifurcation of the river, the fish population theoretically divides in corresponding proportions. Furthermore, spawning fish migrating upstream, and their pursuing predators, arrive at the downstream sites first. With fish-fence technology, a downstream group may block fishes from proceeding upstream.

Researchers from the Colombian Uaupés have noted this distinction in riverine resources. According to Christine Hugh-Jones, "Towards the headwaters the availability of fish gradually declines . . . those who live in the headwaters are described as 'eaters of tiny fish.' The headwater people are forced to rely more on forest products, not necessarily because these are more abundant, but because the fish are scarce" (1979: 239).

Hugh-Jones offers a further distinction: she associates downstream sites with "political dominance," which she attributes to greater involvement in ceremonial exchange. This, in turn, she explains through the "superior cultivation" of downriver settlements (1979: 239). While Hugh-Jones accurately notes the connections among political relations, exchange rituals, and a surplus of the garden products manioc and coca, she overestimates the differences in the quality of cultivable land and overlooks a more critical variable: the capacity to attract labor. Agricultural land is equally or more available to upriver settlements, which are smaller in size, than to larger, more permanent downriver settlements. The ability to mobilize the labor to create an abundance of labor-intensive agricultural products increases a group's capacity for participation in exchange rituals.

The spatial distribution of ranked groups places high-ranked groups downriver and low-ranked groups upriver. The Brazilian Uaupés (downriver) is inhabited by the highest-ranked sibs and their accompanying servant sibs. My own focus reflects the emphasis placed on rank by the chiefly sibs with which I worked. The deemphasis on rank in studies of the Colombian (upper) Uaupés may be attributed to the absence of high-ranked groups in that area. It appears likely that rank structures will be preserved where differences in rank exist and privileges relating to rank are at stake. This observation at once supports and explains Christine Hugh-Jones' "missing" chiefly and servant sibs: they are not located upriver. Furthermore, the Wanano data suggest that the chiefly groups are corporate, or at least "fixed," in terms of riverine territory.

The Dynamics of Rank

Although this study focuses on observations derived from one ranked society, its main purpose is to make observations that are generalizable to other ranked societies as well. For example, a characteristic noted among rank societies elsewhere is geographic or cyclical variation, to the extent that seemingly different political models are found within a single cultural entity. The Northwest Amazon typifies this type of society but exhibits "hierarchical zoning": upriver groups maintain an ideology of hierarchy with few manifestations of it; downriver groups, however, are immersed in the day-to-day practice of ranking.

Gaps in our understanding of the Northwest Amazon as a "ranked" system have stemmed in part from the fact that each individual study has treated its group as a closed system, without fully taking into account the interdependencies and fluxes characterizing the larger socioeconomic whole. Furthermore, previous Uaupés studies have focused only on upriver settlements, which demonstrate, but do not emphasize, ranking. The earlier reports are by no means anomalous or incorrect. They are, however, insufficient. Without a consideration of the downriver chiefly groups, a comprehensive understanding of Uaupés political, economic, and social systems cannot be achieved. This work is the first to be based upon data gathered in downriver (eastern) settlements. Furthermore, the study is aimed at the interactions of widely disparate ranked persons and groups. Specifically, it considers in some detail chiefly sibs and servant sibs living in symbiotic relation to one another. In summary, I find that the weak emphasis on rank upriver—and its strong emphasis downriver—suggests a holistic model for Uaupés society that encompasses patterns of variation and enables us to offer general statements about such societies.

PART I: HISTORY

Chapter 2. European Expansion, Intertribal Relations, and Linguistic Exogamy in the Upper Rio Negro from 1616

THE IMPACT OF EUROPEAN EXPANSION in the Northwest Amazon long preceded the permanent presence of Europeans in the area. As early as 1616 the Dutch had established trading posts in the upper Essequibo River valley, near the present border between Brazil and Guyana. From these bases, Dutch trading reached deep into the Branco and Negro river valleys, exchanging manufactured products such as fish hooks, knives, and needles for Indian slaves.

Dutch monopoly over slaving in this vast area lasted more than a century, its success due not to the coercive force of the Dutch but to the trade relations established with Carib inhabitants who supplied them with war captives.

Whatever tribal enmities existed prior to the Dutch were distended and transformed by their presence. One after another European power fostered and mobilized traditional hostilities. More complex relations and animosities among Carib nations and Arawakan-speaking neighbors gave way, across these river valleys, to the prevailing and simplified relations of captor and captive.

Holland at this time was a major challenger to Portugal in Brazil, having captured two principal Atlantic ports between 1624 and 1630.[1] To counter the Dutch influence in the northern territories, the Portuguese, proceeding northwest along the Rio Negro, formed alliances with a number of traditional enemies of the Dutch-allied Caribs.

Relying heavily on extensive native trade networks, Dutch slaving required few Dutch frontier agents to secure valuable Indian labor power for their Caribbean coastal plantations. Portuguese slaving, in contrast, employed armed troops of official royal expeditionaries, whose activities resulted in the extermination of countless native inhabitants.

In these earliest stages of commercial contact, the Portuguese sought Indian labor to serve as paddlers, often in subsequent slaving expeditions, and in the collection of forest products. Forest spices or *drogas do sertão* including *canela,* a New World substitute for the cinnamon of Ceylon,[2] were among the few lucrative products exported by Pará, the Portuguese colony at the mouth of the Amazon. In an effort to supply their voracious colonists with captive Indian labor, the Portuguese devastated nearly all the native populations along the lower Amazon and its tributaries. Having depleted the river margin of most of its inhabitants, and driven the survivors deep into the interfluve, the Portuguese proceeded into the upper tributary areas.

By the early eighteenth century Portuguese slaving expeditions regularly entered the upper Rio Negro and its affluents. By 1730 the first official slaving expedition, led by Lourenço Belfort, Estacio Rodrigues, and Pedro de Braga, entered the Uaupés River basin. So extensive was slaving in these upriver hinterlands that, despite an official abolition of slavery by Portugal in 1750, the Jesuit Father Ignacio Szentmartonyi estimated that in the single decade between 1740 and 1750 twenty thousand Indians from the upper Rio Negro were enslaved by Portuguese (Szentmartonyi, trans. in Wright 1981). "Whole tribes which were prominent in the upper Rio Negro region at the time of the first European penetration were gone by the 1760's" (Wright 1981: 134).

The Negro and Orinoco River Basins

One of the locations where competition for influence over northern South America was played out most fiercely was the upper Rio Negro/Orinoco drainage divide. The present border between Venezuela and Brazil, still disputed today, reflects three centuries of conflict.[3]

From the Spanish point of view, the presence of the Portuguese in the upper Rio Negro valley brought these colonial competitors within reach of the Orinoco basin, long considered by the Spanish to be within their territories and linked by a natural watercourse to the Rio Negro system.

Europeans first discovered that watercourse, known as the Casiquiare Canal, when Portuguese slavers in the upper Rio Negro ventured unknowingly into the Orinoco, where they encountered the Spanish missionary Father Manuel Román in 1744.[4] Since then, the presence of that watercourse and the strategic possibilities it allowed have been an issue of importance to both the Spanish and the Portuguese.

Concerned about Portuguese encroachment into what were considered Spanish territories, in 1753 the Spanish dispatched an Expedition of Limits, which included a fleet of warships, to secure their possessions in the Orinoco valley and to preclude Portuguese advancement into the area.

Several accounts provide us with a picture of population movements in the Orinoco area of Venezuela in the eighteenth century. These accounts rely heavily upon the correspondence of José Solano, Spanish captain of the Royal Expedition (1753–1760). Expeditionaries arriving in the basin at mid-century encountered four powerful Arawakan-speaking groups engaged in warfare against Caribspeaking and Arawakan-speaking tribes of the Orinoco. Of the four Arawakan tribes, three had allied themselves with the Portuguese: the Manão, the Manetibitano, and the Marabitana. The three groups were renowned for supplying the Portuguese with great numbers of slaves in the upper Rio Negro valley (Wright 1981; Ramos Pérez 1946; Humboldt 1852). Spanish strategy was to gain allies among the indigenous inhabitants who opposed the Portuguese and tip the balance of power in their favor. They therefore set about to win the confidence of the fourth of these warring groups, the non-allied Guaipunave.

According to reports from Ramos Pérez (1946: 312, 313) "With the goal of securing the Santa Fé road . . . , Solano convinced [the Guaipunave leader] Cucero of the need to subdue the Parrenes Indians, who lived at the confluence of the Ariarí." In this he was assisted by the Jesuits, who had been expelled from the Portuguese Amazon and who opposed Portuguese slaving activities. According to Humboldt,

> The arrival of a small body of Spaniards in 1756, under the order of Solano, awakened suspicion in this chief [Cuseru] of the Guaypunave. He was on the point of attempting a contest with them, when the Jesuits convinced him that it would be in his interest to remain at peace with the Christians. Whilst dining at the table of the Spanish general, Cuseru was allured by promises, and the prediction of the approaching fall of his enemies. From being a king he became the mayor of a village; and consented to settle with his people at the new mission of San Fernando de Atabapo [at the confluence of the Atabapo and Guaviare rivers]. (Humboldt 1852: 2:334, 335)

With the assistance of the Spanish, the Guaipunave were able to exterminate the Portuguese-allied Manetibitano from the banks of the Guainía (Codazzi 1940: 24) and then to conquer and displace the Caribs on the Orinoco. From their homeland in the Inírida Valley, the Guaipunave eventually achieved military dominance over all the villages of the Orinoco throughout the mid-eighteenth century (Humboldt 1852: 2:334).

Native inhabitants were conquered for two purposes: slaving and colonizing. Intent upon holding their positions in the Orinoco and Negro valleys, the Spanish and Portuguese established a number of fortified villages between the years 1756 and 1766 and colonized them with Indians who would pledge allegiance to their respective crowns. The Guaipunave Indians were supplied with arms and settled into a large fortified settlement in 1759 at San Fernando de Atabapo, near the confluence of the Orinoco, Guaviare, and Atabapo rivers (see fig. 2). Two years later, in 1761, the Portuguese removed and resettled Tukanoan and Arawakan-speaking Indians of diverse languages to a military outpost at São Gabriel da Cachoeira (known formerly as Uaupés), situated at the confluence of the Uaupés River with the Rio Negro (Bruzzi 1977: 17–18).

Through such forced resettlement of native populations, the Spanish and Portuguese were able to establish and hold their positions along the drainage divide that was to define the boundaries of modern Latin American nations.

Chiefdoms

The Guaipunave, like the three Portuguese-allied Arawakan groups, consisted of federations of settlements united under a single leader. Two Guaipunave chiefs, Macapu and Cuceru, are credited with having led the decisive Orinoco campaign (Codazzi 1940: 24). Chiefs are also reported for each of the Portuguese-allied Arawakan groups: Chief Inão of the Manão, Chief Immon (Ymmon, also Immu) of the Manetibitano, and Chief Cocuí (Cocuý) of the Marabitana. These leaders are alleged to have been hereditary chiefs; more important for this analysis is the agreement among chroniclers that the chiefs were able to ally several groups under their leadership. Giovanni Codazzi, for example, describes paramount chiefs "who rule[d] over certain tribes . . . between which there is an alliance" (1940: 24; my translation).

The concentration of competing chiefdoms located within the Orinoco theater of European competition strongly suggests that these chiefdoms were a product of conditions attached to the European presence. As native populations were brought within European rivalries, low-level local disputes were fueled into predatory relations without regional precedent. Historical evidence strongly suggests two important consequences: first, the consolidation of groups into confederations under military leadership; and, second, a re-

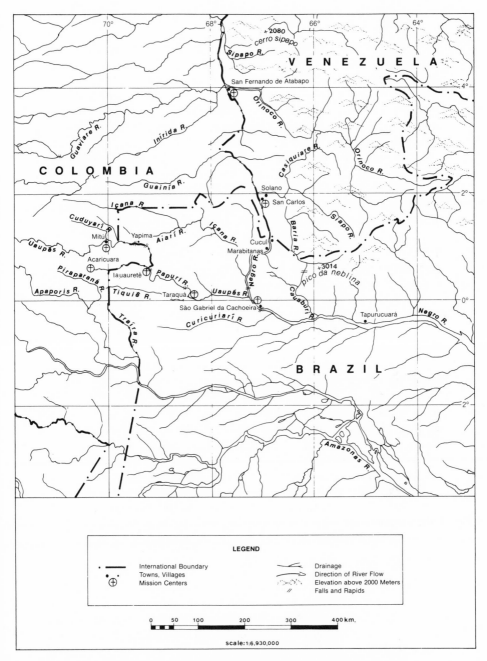

Figure 2. Central Northwest Amazon and environs: Uaupés, Içana, and western Orinoco river basins. Copyright 1992 by Janet M. Chernela.

lated dynamic of population movements, displacements, and forced migrations.

European penetration, then, not only encouraged the creation of paramount chiefdoms, but also set in motion population movements that had an impact upon the entire upper Rio Negro region. The Baniwa, for example, related to the Guaipunave, are thought to have been driven into their present locations on the Aiarí (a short distance overland from the Wanano) from the Guaviare section of the Orinoco basin.

Paramount chiefs have been cited for both groups of Arawakans presently living among the Tukanoans in the Uaupés region: the Baniwa and the Tariana. Robin Wright, for example, names several prominent Arawakan chiefs, among them the Baniwa chief Keroaminali and the Tariana chief Bernardo (1981: 250, 252). William McGovern refers to a Tariana paramount chief at Iauaretê by the name of Nicolão as "overlord" to at least twenty-five different Tariana settlements (1927: 112).[5]

Both the Tariana and Baniwa are linked to the Wanano and to other Eastern Tukanoan groups through marriage ties. The present Wanano in-law relationship with the Arawakan Baniwa of the Aiarí tributary of the Içana River was known at the beginning of this century. Theodor Koch-Grünberg, who visited the area between 1903 and 1905, observed frequent "trade and reciprocal marriages" between Wanano and the Arawakan tribes of the Aiarí (1909: 2:61, 62). He reports locations of Baniwa on the Aiarí, overland north of the Wanano, as well as on the Uaupés, at the mouth of the Querarí. The latter Baniwa settlement separated the Wanano, according to Koch-Grünberg, into an upriver and a downriver branch (1909: 2:66).

While I lived in Yapima, two of the eight in-marrying wives were Tariana. (Chapter 6 presents a song composed by two Tariana wives.) A Baniwa wife had recently passed away, and her two adolescent daughters were sent to her natal village on the Aiarí to marry her Baniwa nephews.

Oral Histories on Warfare and Alliance in the Uaupés Basin

Oral histories I gathered among Wanano reflect their view of history over the past few centuries as it is recounted from generation to generation.[6] While some of these reports have been corroborated among Piratapuya and Arapaço speakers, I carried out no oral histories among Baniwa or Tariana.

In the following discussion on conflict and alliance between different social units, I am interested in two kinds of linkages between groups: marriage and extended kinship. The units of analysis I use include the sib, a localized descent group;[7] the language group, comprised of sibs who share a common putative ancestor and speak one language; and the language family, comprised of related member language groups.[8] For example, Arawakan is the language family to which the Baniwa and Tariana "language groups" belong. Each, in turn, is composed of sibs, or descent-groups, which are typically localized in a single settlement. Likewise, Eastern Tukanoan is the language family to which Wanano and Cubeo "language groups" belong and each, too, is subdivided into named, localized member sibs.

According to Wanano informants, confederacies of Baniwa sibs and accompanying non-Baniwa allies conducted raids throughout the Querarí, Uaupés, Cuiubí, Papurí, and Tiquié rivers. Moreover, several types of alliances are reported, including Baniwa-Tariana, Baniwa-Cubeo, and Baniwa-Wanano alliances.[9] The geographic extent of this raiding is considerable. Campaigns associated with Baniwa leadership, for example, covered an area extending from the Querarí and Içana rivers to the Papurí and Tiquié. Although the actual degree of destruction remains unclear, accounts of settlement relocation from informants of several language groups are consistent. As reported by Wanano informants, raiding and warfare were so severe that numerous villages on the Aiarí affluent of the Içana and the Uaupés rivers were surrounded by spiked trenches.[10]

Confederacies and War Chiefs

Wanano report that several groupings of sibs united under Baniwa and Tariana paramount chiefs for purposes of warfare. Although the duration of leadership and the scope of authority attached to the leadership position beyond specific military goals are difficult to evaluate, a salient feature of such campaigns is the role of a war chief in unifying diverse sibs and recruiting a force of nonkin warriors. Informants recounted the careers of memorable military leaders. For example, the Baniwa Nyapia Taro Pona,[11] in-laws of the Wanano, were renowned for their powerful war chief Maha Wudua (Macaw Face) who reputedly recruited boys from nearby settlements on the Aiarí River to bolster raiding parties.[12] Two other Arawakan Baniwa groups, the Curipaca Wipi Pona and the Buʔsa Dita Parenoa, were also reported to have had chiefs who allied unrelated sibs and enlisted warriors.

Informants agree that raiding for wives was a widespread practice among all Uaupés groups. Such raids were typically limited to a small party of bachelor kinsmen armed with spears and bows and arrows. Young girls were captured and taken as wives. In escalations of raiding, boys were also captured or killed. Escalations of this kind have been attributed to European slavers, since captives could be traded to them in exchange for money or manufactured items.

Oral histories also provide evidence of warring both for captives and for territory. The Wipi Pona, a sib of the Baniwa subgrouping Curipaca, carried out extensive raiding campaigns in which warriors from several Içana groups remained away from their villages for long periods.[13] The Wipi Pona allied with another Baniwa group, the Bu?sa Dita Parenoa, and fought against Baniwa sibs such as the Wayu Pina, as well as against the Tukano and other Eastern Tukanoan groups. Eventually, the Curipaca Wipi Pona lost their hold on their former settlements along the Içana River and sought refuge in the headwater regions of the Guainía in Venezuela. Apparently, other Baniwa sibs occupied the former Wipi Pona sites.

Accounts suggest several alliances of changing constituency. For example, Wanano informants report that only three or four generations ago the Baniwa sib Bu?sa Dita Parenoa (of the Aiarí) formed an alliance with a prominent Tariana sib, the Maha Yücüria. In another configuration, the Bu?sa Dita Parenoa led a grouping of sibs of different language groups, including the Cubeo Maca Pino Pona (of the Querarí River) in widespread raiding among Wanano, Siriano, Tukano, as well as other Cubeo. From their territories on the Querarí and Aiarí rivers to the north and west of the Wanano, they ventured overland as far south as the Papurí River. Raiding expeditions are said to have spanned several years.

Reports on Tariana raiding are numerous but far less specific. Wanano informants support William McGovern (1927) in their accounts that the Tariana moved northward up the Uaupés from its confluence with the Rio Negro. Entering the Uaupés, the Tariana proceeded upriver, displacing the Tukanoan Arapaço, Piratapuya, Miriti-Tapuya, and Tukano in their path. These events must have occurred over two hundred years ago. Even so, the Arapaço, Tukano, and Piratapuya, with whom I worked, knew the precise locations and names of their former villages on the Uaupés. These sites are still regarded by members of these groups as belonging to them, although today the settlements are inhabited by Tariana.[14] The few remaining Miriti-Tapuya (less than 100 people) live inland along feeder streams of the Tiquiê River. The Tariana presently occupy all principal locations on the lower and middle Uaupés, with Tariana settlements reaching as far north as the most downriver Wanano settlement.

The southernmost downriver Wanano settlements reported by

Curt Nimuendajú in 1927 (1950: 162—Tayaçú-Poço and Periquito) are now inhabited by Tariana. A Baniwa settlement to the north of the Brazilian Wanano serves as a wedge in dividing the Wanano into two branches: an upriver, Colombian branch, and downriver, Brazilian branch (Koch-Grünberg 1909: 2:66). The present-day locations of Arawakan settlements to the north (Baniwa) and to the south of the Wanano (Tariana) suggest a pincerlike advancement of Arawakans into the middle Uaupés basin.

Warfare: Summary

Oral histories suggest, then, that two waves of Arawakan expansion continued into contemporary history: groups of Baniwa spreading southward and westward over land and Tariana movement upriver from the Rio Negro into the Uaupés.

According to Wanano informants, confederacies of Baniwa sibs and accompanying non-Baniwa allies conducted raids throughout the Querarí, Uaupés, Papurí, and Tiquiê rivers. On the lower Uaupés, Tariana moving northwest displaced the Eastern Tukanoan Piratapuya, Arapaço, Tukano, and Mirití-Tapuya groups.

Two of the four groups displaced by the Tariana, the Arapaço and the Piratapuya, are considered by the Wanano to be phratric groups. Even so, I have no reports of Wanano fighting to support these brother groups.

Arawakan expansion has been accompanied by assimilation to Tukano culture and full integration into the Tukanoan social universe. As stated, the Tariana and Baniwa are now linked by marriage to Eastern Tukanoan groups.

History and Social Organization:
The Bases for Confederation and Alliance

Brotherhoods

The Wanano recognize four other language groups as extended kin: the Piratapuya, Arapaço, Tuyuka, and Siriano. Together, the five groups may be said to constitute a "phratry" or brotherhood. Wanano report no intraphratric warfare or raiding.[15] Nor do they report coming to the aid of these fraternal groups on the basis of stipulated brotherhood ties.

It is interesting to note, however, that among the Wanano, the Wiroa subgroup—referred to as "slaves" or "servants"—are said to have a separate origin. There is some suggestion that the Wiroa are newcomers to the Wanano, possibly incorporated through warfare. Even so, the Wanano firmly deny any extension of kinship ties on the basis of warfare.

The Arawakan Curipaca sib Wipi Pona offers a different type of strategy. According to Wanano informants, the Wipi Pona carried out long raiding campaigns for which they recruited numerous non-Curipaca warriors on whom they conferred the status of "brother." The Wanano strongly criticize the Curipaca practice of extending brotherhood status to war allies. From the Wanano point of view, the proper basis for alliance in warfare is marriage (Chernela 1989b, 1992).

Marriage

Marriage was achieved through two conventional means: negotiation and seizure. Tukanoan marriage gives rise to a counterclaim that may be the occasion of war if not fulfilled. Complementing the far-reaching incest regulations that prohibit marriage within the language group is the obligation to take wives from alien groups. A daughter given requires that one be given in return. Wife-stealing—a negative exchange—was a commonplace alternative to negotiation. Indeed, marriage raids were ritualized war—marriage and war in this sense being transformations of one another. Such small-scale raiding for women typified Wanano history.

Marriage as Treaty. While marriage in which a wife was taken could initiate war, marriage in which a wife was given could bring about peace. Informants recount wife-giving as one means of ending disputes. For example, warring between Desana and Wanano is said to have ceased when the Desana "gave a woman" to the Wanano. In another instance, an in-law relationship was seen as tantamount to treaty. Speaking of a Baniwa in-law sib, one informant said, "The people of Wamu Macama [sib] were our ancestors' brothers-in-law; for this reason they did not eat Wanano flesh." From the Wanano point of view, in-law status exempted them from Baniwa Wamu Macama aggression. The Wanano still use an intimate nickname to refer to the ancestor who first married a woman of that sib and thus brought about peace.

Co-raiding with In-Laws. A significant feature of the numerous oral history accounts is the repeated mention of the Baniwa having enlisted Wanano young men in their wars against Baniwa enemies. Wanano informants attribute their participation to in-law obligation. One informant expressed it this way: "Since our grandfathers were brothers-in-law of the Baniwa, they carried them to help in a war at the headwaters of the Papurí River and also in the Cuiubí and Querarí rivers. In these rivers, the Baniwa went together with our ancestors killing people." As in-laws of the Baniwa, the Wanano participated in campaigns against the Cubeo, the Tukano, and other Baniwa groups. It must be noted that the Cubeo and Tukano also stand in in-law relation to the Wanano—a point that reflects the varying degrees of in-lawhood and their vacillations throughout history.

Discussion: Chiefdoms and Warfare

Political consolidation is diagnostic in distinguishing a ranked society from a chiefdom. A ranked society is a society without government: "In a rank(ed) society leaders can lead, but followers may not follow. Commands are given, but sometimes they may not be obeyed" (Fried 1967: 133). In contrast, a chiefdom is described as "an autonomous political unit comprising a number of communities under the permanent control of a paramount chief" (Carneiro 1991: 168).

Informants distinguished between relatively small-scale "raiding in sibs," as in wife capture, and the temporary union of several sibs under the common leadership of a single chief. The reports confirm the potential for recognition of leadership above the sib level by otherwise autonomous local groups. In some cases, heads were apparently able to rally support beyond their own sib units. However, the confederations that reportedly cohered under a paramount chief occurred mainly among Arawakan Tariana and Baniwa subdivisions. If, as evidence suggests, Arawakan-speaking groups moved westward from the Rio Negro area toward the Uaupés basin, they would have conquered and displaced populations formerly occupying those areas. We have evidence of this on the lower and middle Uaupés, where the Arawakan-speaking Tariana and Baniwa displaced numerous settlements of Eastern Tukanoan–speaking groups. There is strong evidence, then, to suggest that the Arawakan groups in the area were expanding chiefdoms when they entered the Uaupés.

While Wanano informants vividly recall Arawakan war chiefs and campaigns, they have no such recollection of their own campaigns. On the other hand, it is evident that the Wanano provided warriors to the Baniwa in what the Wanano consider to be "Baniwa wars." These data suggest several important conclusions. For one thing, we must now reconsider the Wanano as constituents of a regional-based chiefdom in which Arawakan leadership predominated. By providing warriors and wives to the Baniwa, the Wanano succeeded in maintaining most of their settlement sites on the hotly contested Uaupés River. This is supported by the fact that the Tariana and Baniwa, who displaced numerous Arawakan and Eastern Tukanoan settlements elsewhere, displaced few Wanano settlements. This is especially noteworthy since the Wanano are located between the Baniwa, moving south, and the Tariana, moving north.

The difference between the terms "chiefdom" and "ranked society" used in models of political organization lies in the degree of political consolidation of chiefdoms. The history of Uaupés intertribal warfare suggests that some groups formed politically consolidated units under paramount chiefs, while other groups created affinal linkages to those units. The Uaupés case shows that horizontal extension—in the form of marriage alliance—is as viable and resilient a form as political consolidation.

Conclusion

In summary, then, the Wanano recognize three primary sets of equivalences that define group relations: fraternal, in which no women are exchanged; war, in which a woman is taken; and treaty, in which a woman is given.

Wanano do not report conflicts with member groups of their own phratry, nor do they report aiding another group on the basis of brotherhood ties. Instead, informants express strong disapproval of groups that form brotherhoods of independent language groups on the basis of warfare. The Curipaca Wipi Pona sib was reported to confer brotherhood status on allies, subjecting phratric relation to pragmatic considerations. For the Wanano, brotherhood is affirmed as "natural," distinguished from the artifice of marriage.

Although there is evidence of Wanano brotherhoods resulting from warfare, there is no acknowledgment of this in practice. On the other hand, warfare and alliance are inextricably related to the exchange of women in both idea and in practice.

For the Eastern Tukanoan, the ties produced by warfare are the ties of marriage, not kinship. Whatever kin-ordered vertical consolidation occurs is mystified by ideology. Instead, transformations of warfare in the form of horizontal, affinal linkages are maintained. These linkages are institutionalized in several ways: by the incest rule stating that marriages may only take place outside the language group; by the practice of ongoing affinity with a given language group; and by a body of oral literature that legitimizes and justifies through citing ancestral precedents.

In the multilingual Northwest Amazon there is no "standard" language. Instead, other languages equal mother-languages and are negatively evaluated by the speaker-descendants of any one language. The devaluation of mother's language, shared by the entire linguistic community, appears more reasonable when it is remembered that wives were historically foreigners captured in war. Moreover, if offspring spoke the enemy language of their mothers, the patrilanguage might eventually be eradicated.

The fundamental opposition between a wife freely given and a wife forcibly taken is the balance between social contract and war. Marriage is both the product of war and the management of conflict. A woman taken is war; a woman given is treaty. War and marriage are transformations of one another, part of a continuum of cultural practices that are touched off situationally as in-laws are feasted, guested, and raided; raided, guested, and feasted.

The Wanano have no supralocal military organizations with which to defend their borders. Instead, they pay for peace with women. Marriage—loose, egalitarian affinities rather than internal consolidation—is their overriding strategy.

Chapter 3. Scientific and Missionary Activities in the Uaupés Basin from 1760

The Eighteenth Century

THE THREAT OF SPANISH INCURSION into the upper Rio Negro region in the early 1760s inspired the Portuguese further to fortify their presence. In 1764 they sent reconnaissance expeditions up the Uaupés and its tributaries and dispatched troops as far as Ipanorê, an island located 70 km downriver from the Wanano. Ipanorê was to become the focus of mission and trade activities for the next two centuries.

In 1790 André Fernandes de Souza, the parish priest of São Gabriel, gathered tribal inhabitants from various Tukanoan- and Arawakan-speaking groups into a large settlement at Ipanorê (Aranha 1907). By 1795 de Souza had baptized 669 Indians (de Souza 1848: 465–466; cited in Wright 1981: 168). The settlement became so large that one writer called the Ipanorê of 1883 "the capital of all Uaupés and Paporí villages." "Ipanorê . . . was the village that possessed the largest number of houses and inhabitants. Besides the church, which was, in architecture and proportion, the largest and best of any on this river, it also had a cemetery, school, missionary residence, and jail" (Henri Coudreau, in Aranha 1907: 33, 58; my translation).

Ipanorê and São Gabriel were among the many population centers or *aldeias* to which Indians were recruited by force to work for the Portuguese. The basis of the *aldeia* system, as stated in an Indian statute of 1709, refers to the removal of Indians as "persuasions" and provides three objectives: to provide a downriver labor force for the colonists; to gather forest products upriver; and to defend the crown's territories. Indians were drawn into such controlled settlements, where they were available as a labor reservoir to the crown or to colonists (Chernela 1988b, 1989b).

Although the law specifies payment for Indian labor, wages were negligible. Typical compensation for one month's labor in the mid-eighteenth century was a bulk of cloth. Indians were then required to wear the cloth to establish themselves as "civil."

Indigenous inhabitants were forcibly moved or "persuaded" to descend to such settlements, where they were supplied with European arms and trade goods. In the settlements they would be schooled in Portuguese language and culture, given Portuguese surnames, trained and encouraged in techniques of intensive agriculture, policed, and generally educated in the ways of the Europeans.

From the late eighteenth until the early twentieth century, the Portuguese attempted to resettle the Indians of the Içana, Uaupés, and Xié at such posts, by means of *descimentos* or downriver recruitments. The Indians often resented and resisted such policies. In 1782 and 1783 Indians resisting resettlement deserted many settlements on the lower Uaupés (Wright 1981: 155). By 1820 the indigenous population of the Rio Negro was dramatically reduced (Lopes de Sousa 1959: 205).

The massive recruitment, relocation, and sedentarization of New World populations was organized over three centuries for the economic and political goals of the Iberian powers. Yet while the Spanish and the Portuguese both engaged in forced migrations, shifting massive populations for strategic and profitable ends, the Spanish attached the Indian population to the soil, while the Portuguese removed the Indian population. While agricultural enterprises such as coffee, cotton, indigo, and cocoa were attempted in the Lusitanian Amazon, the resource of greatest economic value to the colonial Portuguese was labor.

Following the Treaty of Madrid in the mid-eighteenth century, which defined Spanish and Portuguese New World possessions, a number of royal geographical expeditions were dispatched to map and explore the hinterlands. Captain João Pereira Caldas headed the first of these official geographic explorations in 1781 (Rondón 1969: 154). In 1784 Manoel Da Gamma Lobo d'Almada explored the Uaupés for demarcation purposes; soon thereafter, Alexandre Rodrigues Ferreira, a Brazilian naturalist, conducted an extensive mapping expedition in order to evaluate the region's economic potential. Despite these efforts, knowledge of the Uaupés region remained sketchy in comparison to better traveled, more accessible tributaries of the Rio Negro.

The Nineteenth Century: Scientific Travel and Missionary Activity

Wallace and Spruce

The nineteenth century produced the first detailed European reports on the Uaupés. Two Englishmen, the prominent naturalist Alfred

Russel Wallace and the botanist Richard Spruce, made lengthy visits to the Uaupés region between 1851 and 1853, writing accounts that were remarkable for their detailed observations.

Spruce's expeditions took him as far upriver as Iauaretê (he was never to enter the Wanano area), where he provided critical pioneering data on local flora and on the river's flooding patterns. Although he made few ethnographic remarks, he did recount visits among the Arawakan Baré on the Rio Negro south of São Gabriel and described a po?oa exchange ceremony (1908: 1:312–315). He also described the presence of a Tariana paramount chief at Iauaretê (1908: 1:324).

Wallace's first trip in 1851 took him as far upriver as Iauaretê, where he attended and described an exchange dance in a large communal longhouse or maloka. He observed that over three hundred people were present and at least fifty panpipes were played (Wallace 1969: 202–205). The ceremony he describes, including a mock spear battle, coincides remarkably with the po?oa exchange ceremony as it is enacted today (discussed in chapter 8).

Entering the Wanano region in 1852, Wallace refers to the Anana tribe; later, translating anana from língua geral, he calls them the "Pineapple" tribe. In the lower part of the Wanano territory he lists numerous settlements: Arara, Miri, Tamaquerie, Paroquet, Iapoo, Tatú, Amana, Camoa, Yanti, and Carurú (1969: 239). Only half of these exist today.

Wallace spent several days at the Wanano settlement of Carurú, where he was struck by the abundance of fish (1969: 241). He later compared this abundance to the paucity of fish and fowl at upriver settlements. He describes Carurú as comprised of a large longhouse (maloka) and smaller houses. "The front of the maloka was painted very tastefully in diamonds and circles, with red, yellow, white, and black" (1969: 240). Wallace's account of Carurú also describes a boy's initiation ceremony and includes careful sketches of petroglyphs at the settlement.

After his stay in Carurú, the river and difficulties of passage absorbed Wallace's attention: he seldom mentions settlements or Indians. Wallace's descriptions of the river are detailed:

> The river from Jauarite may be said to average about a third of a mile wide, but the bends and turns are innumerable; and at every rapid it almost always spreads out into such deep bays, and is divided into channels by so many rocks and islands, as to make one sometimes think that the water is suddenly flowing back in a direction contrary to that it had previously been taking. Caruru Caxoeira itself is greater than any we had yet seen,—rushing

amongst huge rocks down a descent of perhaps fifteen or twenty feet. The only way of passing this, was to pull the canoe over the dry rock, which rose considerably above the level of the water, and was rather rugged, being interrupted in places by breaks or steps two or three feet high. (1969: 239–240)

Wallace did not hesitate to comment on Indian-white relations. He reported on the raiding and enslavement that characterized the mid-nineteenth century (1969: 10–12), recording numerous instances of exploitation.

Wallace identifies a lieutenant of the National Guard, Jesuino Cordeiro, as a force in the mid-century slave trade. On his arrival at Uaracapury (Colombia), Wallace observes: "There was hardly a male in the village, messrs. Jesuino and Chagas having taken them all with them up the river, to assist in an attack on an Indian tribe, the Carapanas, where they had hoped to get a lot of women, boys, and children to take as presents to Barra [Manaus]" (1969: 250–251).

He writes, "On the 4th [April 4, 1852] . . . Senhors Jesuino and Chagas arrived with a whole fleet of canoes, and upwards of twenty prisoners, all, but one, women and children. Seven men and one woman had been killed; the rest of the men escaped" (1969: 252).

Wallace notes complicity from several sources in the procurement and trade of young Indians:

> The "negociantes" and authorities in Barra [Manaus] and Pará, ask the traders among the Indians to procure a boy or a girl for them, well knowing the only manner in which they can be obtained; in fact, the Government in some degree authorizes the practice. There is something to be said too in its favour, for the Indians make war on each other,—principally the natives of the margin of the river on those in the more distant igaripes— for the sake of their weapons and ornaments, and for revenge of any injury, real or imaginary, and then kill all they can, reserving only some young girls for their wives. The hope of selling them to the traders, however, induces them to spare many who would otherwise be murdered. These are brought up to some degree of civilization (though I much doubt if they are better or happier than in their native forests) . . . Senhor L. [a merchant trader] had been requested by two parties at Barra—one the Delegarde de Policia—to furnish them each with an Indian girl . . . , as this man was an old hand at the business. (1969: 207)

Spruce also observed slaving, specifically among the Arawakan Carapana: ". . . the Brazilian government has promulgated edicts against the seizing of the native inhabitants and reducing them to slavery yet the practice still exists and is carried out. I speak of this with certainty because since I came up the Rio Negro two such expeditions have been sent up a tributary of the Uaupés, called the Rio Papurís, to make pegas [captures] among the Carapana Indians . . . I have also seen and conversed with two female children stolen from the Carapanas in these expeditions" (1908: 1:355–356).

As director of Indians of the Uaupés and Içana, Cordeiro was charged with "civilizing the Cubeo, Uanana, and Umaua populations of the Upper Uaupés" (Rondón 1969: 155). One of his primary efforts was enticing Indians of the forest interior to resettle on the main banks of the river. He forged alliances with Tukano, Tariana, and Mirití chiefs in order to accomplish these ends (Wright 1981: 232–236). Various Indian chiefs resisted this campaign, and in 1853 a group of Carapana attacked a settlement of Cubeo where Cordeiro was staying. Cordeiro personally led an attack against the Carapana with the help of the Cubeo and Wanano (Wright 1981: 248–249). Today only remnants of the former Umaua and Mirití populations remain.

In response to intense provocation, the Indians on the Uaupés, Içana, and Xié formed alliances in the late 1850s and together rebelled. At the same time a Tukano messiah named Alexandre Christu attracted a large following. This implicit threat led the Barra government to appoint seventy-five men—under the leadership of police chief (and municipal justice) Marcos Antonio Rodrigues de Sousa—to investigate and quell the rebellion. Rodrigues never found Alexandre. He did, however, implicate the merchants, military, and missionaries in provoking the uprising and tried to rid the area of the most offensive intruders. This commission's progressive work, completed in September 1858, was undone eight years later when the abolition of the post of director of Indians gave the military and merchants free rein (Wright 1981: 312).

Missionary Activity

During the same period the Wanano area underwent brief but intense missionary activity. In 1845 the governor of Pará issued Decreto e Regulamento No. 426, which mandated "catechization and civilization, education and governing" of all the Amazonian indigenous people (Wright 1981: 228). Four years later the Mission of the Uaupés and Içana was founded, and the governor of Amazonas appointed the first missionary to concentrate in the Wanano region, the Capuchin Frei Gregorio José María de Bene (Bruzzi 1977: 18).[1]

Between 1852 and 1854 de Bene disseminated the catechism from three principal Uaupés bases: São Jerónimo near Ipanorê, Mitú rapids in Colombia, and the Wanano settlement at Carurú. From his Carurú base, de Bene claimed to have gathered some 300 Indians under his tutelage (Koch-Grünberg 1909: 2:7). He visited fifteen villages on the Uaupés (Wright 1981: 233), baptizing 550 people—a quarter of the population with which he made contact. De Bene abandoned his mission on the Uaupés after two years because of disputes with Jesuino Cordeiro, then director of Indians (Koch-Grünberg 1909: 2:8). De Bene's presence on the middle Uaupés therefore had brief, though significant, impact.

The Capuchins continued to dominate missionary activity in the upper Rio Negro and Uaupés areas until the 1880s, when the provincial government invited the Franciscans into the area. Three Franciscans were appointed: Frei Venancio Zilochi, who worked on the Tiquiê; Frei Iluminato José Coppi, who worked on the middle and upper Uaupés, the Papurí, and Ipanorê; and Frei Matheus Camioni, who worked on the lower Uaupés and at Taracua. Their string of posts, spanning some 800 km, allowed river contact with some 3,000 inhabitants (Koch-Grünberg 1909: 2:7–9). Between 1881 and 1883 the missionaries zealously concentrated and organized Indians into large mission centers. One of these was Ipanorê, which then numbered sixty-two houses and contained a jail with separate quarters for men and women. Frei José formed a uniformed police force among the Tariana at Iauaretê.

Koch-Grünberg describes the departure of the missionaries:

> In October of the year 1883: PP. José and Matheus were driven by their overzealousness to a fateful folly: to profane cult items of the Tariana in Ipanorê, which supposedly came within a hair of costing them their lives. They had to flee, and didn't return to the Caiary [Uaupés]. The Brazilian traders, to whom the activity of the missionaries had long been a thorn in the eye, may have had a large part in this exit, because the missions had certainly accorded the poor Indians protection in several connections against the encroachment of the often unscrupulous whites. The converts dispersed themselves and took up their old habits, which had not yet become alien to them. Since this time, the attempt has not been renewed and the present-day Indians have scarcely a vague recollection of the pastors. (1909: 2:10)[2]

Referring to the limited impact of the Franciscans' activity (1808–1883), Koch-Grünberg states: "By the official information, the mission numbered 227 souls in 24 houses in the year 1853" (1909: 2:74); but by 1904 it had been abandoned and returned to scrub forest.

Upriver from the Wanano village of Jutica (which at the time was called Trinidade by the missionaries and numbered eighty-four inhabitants) there were five smaller stations.[3]

The Franciscans had established chapels in no less than twenty-two villages on the Uaupés and its tributaries. These stations were distributed in the regions of the Tukano, Desana, Tariana, Piratapuya, Arapaço, Wanano, Baniwa, Cubeo, and Makú.

Early Twentieth-Century Contact

Koch-Grünberg

The German ethnologist Theodor Koch-Grünberg spent three weeks at Brazilian Wanano settlements in 1904. Like Wallace, Koch-Grünberg traveled to the upriver boundary of Wanano territory at Uaracapury, above the mouth of the Cuduiarí (1909: 2:66–74). His description of the upper Uaupés includes the first detailed, firsthand European account of the Wanano: "The Uanana . . . [number] 500 to 600 souls, who are divided into some 30 settlements. Individual nomadic groups of this tribe are distinguished from the neighbors with special names. Therefore the Tukano on the Tiquiê call the Uanana of the Abiú Igarapé, Uiroa, as distinguished from the real Uanana, the Oxkotikana, and indicated to me another nomadic tribe of the Uanana: the Nixtisoli. In the lingoa geral the Uanana of the Abiú Igarapé, as distinct from the rest of the Uanana, are called Uanana-Tapuyo" (1909: 2:75). His report provides early documentation of the tradition of the Wiroa as a distinct group of Wanano (see chapter 4).

Traveling upriver from Iauareté in 1904, Koch-Grünberg visited the Wanano settlements Jutica (Yapima), Matapí (Bucacopa), Carurú (Mo), and Taracua in Brazil. His descriptions of Brazilian settlements indicate few departures from today's pattern. He mentions a *maloka* at Uruapecuma (1909: 2:64), which he locates between Carurú (Mo) and Jutica (Yapima). This site is no longer inhabited. Because he lists no settlements at the present sites of Tiririca and Bacaba, we may conclude that these sites were not occupied. It is also interesting to note that at the time of his visit Carurú's population size was as high as 200, and the village was already divided into separate family dwellings. He reports nine small habitations and two longhouses on both sides of the river.

Koch-Grünberg reports that Wanano settlement distribution diverged into an upriver and a downriver branch, separated "by tribes who are generally designated by the collective name of Baniwa ... [who] were subjugated by the invading Kubeua [Cubeo] and adopted the language of their conquerors" (1909: 2:66). These groups thus "divide the Uanano into two branches" near the mouth of the Querarí (1909: 2:66). He mentions a Baniwa longhouse at the confluence of the Querarí with the Uaupés. Making further observations about changes in settlement, he holds that the "true land" of the Cubeo proceeds upriver from Taiassu Cachoeira in Colombia, but that "the Uanana settled on the whole stretch and gradually pushed the Kobeua [Cubeo] back upstream" (1909: 2:74). Koch-Grünberg also makes intriguing remarks about Wanano sociopolitical organization. He mentions that a young chief at the downstream village of Carurú (Mo) was "the high chief of the whole Uanano tribe" (1909: 2:147) and that "above the Querary mouth, the second part of the Uanano live in numerous *malocas*. They recognize the chieftaincy in Mo [Carurú] as their high chief (overlord) even if his power is only nominal in these days" (1909: 2:67).

His is not the only suggestion that paramount chiefs existed in the Uaupés (cf. Spruce 1908; McGovern 1927), but it is the only mention of a Wanano paramount chief. One should probably accept these labels with caution. The pattern of ultimate seniority at Mo (Carurú) would conform to the stated ideal that the highest-ranked groups reside downriver and lend support to informants' reports that today's higher-ranked sibs splintered from Mo and moved upstream. Koch-Grünberg also makes several references to hunter-gatherer Makú workers in two high-ranking downriver Wanano settlements, mentioning Makú "slaves" at Bucacopa and Mo (1909: 59–60).

Koch-Grünberg also reports that the Wanano from Mo to Yapima are "in lively communication with the [Baniwa] tribes of the Aiarí" (1909: 2:62), having observed frequent "trade and reciprocal marriages" between them. He describes a mask dance he attended at Bucacopa (Matapí) (1909: 2:61) whose participants were Wanano and Desana. The present Wanano relationship with the Desana of the Papurí and the Arawak Baniwa of the Aiarí apparently reflects a tradition of affinity; at least it was already in existence at the beginning of this century.

At Bucacopa (Matapí) Koch-Grünberg attended a *po?oa* dance in which *mirití* (Mauritia *flexuosa*) fruit was exchanged and notes that it coincides with a ceremony he witnessed on the Tiquié (1909: 2:58). He mentions flutes, which are still used, and dance masks, which are not. His observation that the dance shields that he purchased at Bucacopa had been made by the Desana of the Papurí River further supports ongoing contacts and possible marriage between the Wanano of Bucacopa and the Desana of the Papurí (Bucacopa is the subject of chapter 10).

He also mentions the custom of burying the dead in special cemeteries on islands or in the forest interior. Today the custom persists; the high-ranked sibs bury their dead on an island near Bucacopa; lower-ranked groups bury their dead in the forest interior.

Koch-Grünberg describes the view from the large communal longhouse (*maloka*) at Bucacopa: "From up on the steep height, on which the *maloka* lies, one has an indescribably magnificent view, especially in the soft evening light of the tropical summer. One sees far downstream halfway to Caruru . . . Like natural backdrops, the forested bank peaks project themselves on the curves of the river" (1909: 2:63). He describes the *maloka* at Bucacopa as "a beautiful, spacious house . . . painted with bright designs on the bark covering of the front wall . . . The two middle posts also bore figures in bright colors" (1909: 2:147).

Rubber Trade

Koch-Grünberg's visit occurred at the height of Amazonia's rubber era. He mentions the Wanano intense distrust of whites, which he attributes at least in part to Colombian rubber traders who stole food, captured young boys, and raped and carried off Wanano women (1909: 2:64, 69, 156): ". . . the poor Indians had reason to mistrust the whites, because for half a year, Colombian rubber collectors from the west had appeared on the Upper Caiary [Uaupés] and had arrived at the Uanana villages, where they had behaved evilly. In all the *malokas* we stayed in during this tour, we received bitter complaints about those pioneers of civilization" (1909: 2:145).

Out-Migration

The rubber boom reached the upper Rio Negro in the early 1870s. Rubber collection was confined principally to the *igapó* areas below the Uaupés on the Rio Negro, on the Tiquiê, and in Colombia. The middle Uaupés, where the Wanano lived, was unsuitable for rubber collection. During that time *patrões* collected large numbers of workers from the Uaupés and Içana river valleys (Wright 1981: 324) and carried them to rubber camps. By the early 1900s the adult males of the Wanano, Baniwa, Bará, and Tukano were collecting rubber as far away as the lower Rio Negro.

Rubber collection declined in 1912 and was revived only during

World War II when Asiatic rubber sources were cut off; many Wanano emigrated when wartime demand for rubber created jobs in Colombia and elsewhere. Many remained outside the region in centers in Colombia such as Mitú, Miraflores, and San José del Guaviare, or Puerto Inírida in Venezuela. These opportunities for wage labor continue to draw indigenous peoples out of the region, despite the poor living conditions that generally accompany employment. In the 1970s and 1980s the call to work in Colombia's cocaine fields had a similar depopulating effect.

Nimuendajú

In 1927 Curt Nimuendajú arrived in the same area that Koch-Grünberg had visited in 1904 and found a Wanano population numbering 218 (1950: 145). He distinguished two groups: 50 persons inhabiting five settlements west of the confluence with the Querarí, which he apparently did not visit; and 168 persons dispersed in twelve settlements east of the Querarí. Recalling that Koch-Grünberg encountered 200 people in the single settlement of Mo, the total population and number of persons per settlement is surprisingly low.

During that time the rubber camps had reached their height. Outmigration, slaving, and disease all contributed to a dramatic decline in population. (Koch-Grünberg refers to three "great epidemics" that had decimated the population [1909: 2:24].)

According to contemporary informants, many Wanano fled into the forest during the rubber years. As late as 1927 Colombian rubber collectors descended the Uaupés to take Indians from Brazilian territory (Nimuendajú 1950: 145). Nimuendajú came across one Wanano family taking refuge near in-laws in an isolated encampment on the Aiarí (1950: 142). He also names two whites who became notorious for taking advantage of Indians in the Wanano region: the Peruvian criminal Julio Cesar Barreto, who extended credit for manufactured items and demanded labor as payment; and Antonio Maia, a Brazilian who paid his workers with liquor to maintain the Indians in debt and servitude. In 1927 Antonio Maia was appointed assistant mayor of the entire Brazilian Uaupés territory (Nimuendajú 1950: 144).

Today the eastern Wanano number approximately 600–800. If Nimuendajú's 1927 figure is credible, the population has increased by more than 300 percent. Settlements now contain between 30 and 155 people. The largest settlement observed by Nimuendajú was Jutica (Yapima), which then had only 58 inhabitants (Koch-Grünberg

Table 1. *Settlements Reported by Nimuendajú (1927)*

Place	1927 Population	1979 Population [a]
Carapana	10	uninhabited (or now Baniwa)
Taracua	9	38
Tiririca		7
Taina	7	20
Seringa	9	uninhabited
Yutica	58	77
Capi-Igarape	10	uninhabited
Yacare	10	55
Matapí [b]	14	30
Carurú	34	160
Arara [b]		82
Yandu	13	26
Tayaçú-Poço	10	now Tariana
Periquito	10	now Tariana

[a] Based on author's censuses, conducted in 1978 and 1979. The number of residents in a single settlement varies because of the custom of lengthy "visits" to other settlements.

[b] Today Matapí and Arara are both comprised of sister settlements, situated across the river from one another. The figures here refer only to the settlement in Brazil (on the northern bank).

reports 84 inhabitants for that settlement in 1904). Nimuendajú's listing of population by settlement indicates a total population of only 184 for the eastern Wanano (1950: 162). The mean number of inhabitants in the 12 settlements he lists is 15 people per village. My visits to Uaupés settlements in Brazil indicate that today this would be an extremely low population for any settlement; present settlements average about 50 inhabitants. At the same time, several sites that were visited by Nimuendajú in 1927 are no longer occupied. If the estimates of both Koch-Grünberg (500 to 600) and Nimuendajú (218) are correct, 60 percent of the Wanano population was lost in a 23-year period.

Salesian Mission Activity: 1914 to Present

In 1914 Pope Pius X conferred upon the Salesian order the administration of the Prefeitura Apostólico do Rio Negro (Massa 1933: 43). The Salesians founded mission stations at São Gabriel in 1915, Taracua in 1924, Iauaretê in 1929, and Pari Cachoeira in 1945. The domain of the Salesians extends throughout the Brazilian Uaupés, the Papurí, and the Tiquié. Arriving in the wake of the rubber camp atrocities, the Salesians offered security, safety, and protection against slave raiding.

These major mission bases became religious, educational, and mercantile centers. Several Salesian programs extended Western culture into outlying villages. The mission appointed native "animators" in each village to mediate between the mission center and the villages and to encourage the production of surplus agricultural products and salable craft items to be traded at the mission for manufactured products. They established three large boarding schools and more than sixty day schools that children were obliged to attend. They also appointed native catechists in each village who performed weekly rituals, including a lesson in ethical instruction "correcting" specific indigenous beliefs and practices.

Shortly after their arrival, the Salesians campaigned to alter the traditional habitation from the large multifamily longhouse (*maloka*) to a village of small nuclear family dwellings arranged in lines. By 1956 the only remaining *maloka*s on the Brazilian Uaupés were those of the Wanano and Cubeo—those furthest from the mission centers at Iauaretê and Taracua. However, even in settlements where these changes took hold, traditional patterns of spatial relations—which are of extreme importance to all Tukanoan peoples—remained: the village pattern today recalls the traditional *maloka*. The traditional orientation to river and garden remains intact, with a men's path to the river and a women's path to the gardens. The arrangement of smaller dwellings recreates the spatial relationships of the former nuclear family compartments of the traditional longhouse. Furthermore, the senior member's residence is frequently in the precise location where his compartment would have been in the *maloka*. Although the newer structures are smaller, they often evolve into extended family dwellings housing as many as twelve to fifteen inhabitants; this is the number of inhabitants of many former *maloka*s (for settlement figures, see Goldman 1963; Jackson 1972; C. Hugh-Jones 1979; and S. Hugh-Jones 1979).

Land Demarcation and Calha Norte: 1985

In 1978 at the request of Brazil's Indian protection agency, FUNAI (Fundação Nacional do Indio), the Indians of the Uaupés submitted an official requisition for demarcation of the Indian lands surrounding the Uaupés and its tributaries. Their formal request to the government called for a single integrated indigenous territory, taking into account the special circumstances of interdependencies of the out-marrying descent groups in the area and the multitribal compositions of local settlements. The demarcation was first slowed, and finally interrupted, when a decree placed the border regions of Brazil under special restriction in 1985.

On June 19, 1985, the new civilian president, José Sarney, set in motion an elaborate project for economic development and military defense in the northern borders of the country. Referring to the rivers that drain the frontier region, the project was given the name Calha Norte (northern drainage) and placed under the authority of the National Security Council.

The project includes within its scope 4,000 km to the north of the Amazon-Solimões hydrographic axis along the northern borders shared with Peru, Colombia, Venezuela, Guyana, Surinam, and French Guiana. The total land amounts to 14 percent of Brazil's national territory. Any demarcation of Indian lands falling within these regions, then, is subject to the goals and considerations of the national project.

Approximately ten years after the first official request for an integrated indigenous territory in the upper Rio Negro, a plan was approved that would divide the area into a number of indigenous isolates, designated indigenous "colonies" and "areas." As a result of such partitioning, it has been estimated that the Indians of the Uaupés basin have lost up to 60 percent of the lands formerly occupied and utilized by them.

The allocations "colony" and "area" refer to degree of acculturation. Lands of riverine Indians, such as the Wanano, are designated "colonies," for which development is intended, and forest regions occupied by Makuan hunters are designated "indigenous areas," in which cultural conservation is the stated policy. The indigenous colonies would be a focus for development funding and technical assistance. In these colonies FUNAI would oversee development efforts designed to increase agricultural production and increase Indian participation in national society.

The Brazilian constitution, however, mandates that social organization, customs, languages, beliefs, and traditions of indigenous peoples must be respected and protected, regardless of degree of contact with non-Indian society. The allocation of Indian lands into "colonies" and "areas" has therefore come under some criticism within Brazil.

The remaining interstitial regions lying between indigenous isolates are designated national forests (FLONA) or national parks. In these areas the Indians have "preferential rights" to natural resources, but non-Indian entities, such as mining firms, lumbering firms, or ranchers, are also permitted to exploit these same resources. Although the term "national forest" suggests a highly protected zone, it is, in fact, the least restricted of the area designations. The impact of these recent economic and political policy decisions on indigenous peoples in this region is difficult to predict.

PART II: SOCIOLOGY

Chapter 4. Social Organization

IN THE SOCIAL UNIVERSE in which the Wanano conceptualize themselves, the most inclusive category is the *mahsa*, which encompasses the fifteen to twenty autonomous language groups of the Uaupés basin. Patrilineal descent governs membership in the *mahsa*, which stands in opposition to two other categories: *peogü* and *pehkasü*. The Wanano have given the name *peogü* to the seminomadic hunting peoples of the forest interior who appear in the literature as Makú (Silverwood-Cope 1972; Reid 1979; Ramos et al. 1980). Because they violate the fundamental Uaupés incest taboo by marrying speakers of the same language, the *peogü* are regarded by the Wanano as subhuman, intermediate between human and animal beings. *Pehkasü* is a term that refers to missionaries, river traders, and other outsiders, including anthropological field workers.

The constituent parts of the *mahsa*—the named, exogamous descent groups of the Uaupés—have been referred to in the literature as "tribes" or "language groups." Memberships in these groups are mutually exclusive, founded upon the sole criterion of patrilineal descent. In this way, membership is ancestor-oriented, although ancestors are designated rather than demonstrated.

Each language group is in turn subdivided into units I call sibs. All of these organizational groupings, regardless of level or magnitude, are known by the same Wanano term—*kurua*. The Wanano refer to themselves as being of one *kurua* and view themselves as a group defined primarily by their unique language, name, and distinct ancestral history.

The organization of segments within the larger *mahsa* may be seen as both concentric and dualistic. The structure is concentric in the sense that its component parts are hierarchically structured units of different magnitude. Within each level, groups are ranked in relation to all others by calculation of group placement. It is dualistic in the sense that, from the standpoint of any single *kurua*, all others are either kin or marriageable. The Wanano recognize four other *kurua* as "brother groups" (phratries) and therefore not marriageable: the Piratapuya, Arapaço, Siriano, and Tuyuka. Theoretically all other groups are marriageable, but some lack the established alliances that would make them ongoing in-laws.

Descent Groups: The *Kurua*

The Language Group

The highest-ordered, named group of affiliation is known in the literature as the tribe or language group. (The phratry is unnamed and recognizes no common ancestor.) With some exceptions,[1] the language group is an exogamous unit whose most distinctive feature—to the Indians as well as to outside observers—is its language. The Wanano say that brotherhood is expressed and demonstrated "through common language." I therefore follow Jean Jackson (1974, 1977) in referring to this unit as the language group.[2] Jackson states:

> We can characterize language groups as named patrilineal descent units identified with a specific language (their father-language; Sorensen 1967), the members of which (1) observe a rule of exogamy, (2) terminologically distinguish at this level agnates from other kinsmen, and (3) identify with co-members as "brother people," using a distinct name, language, and certain other differences as boundary-defining markers. These other differences consist of separate semi-mythical founding ancestors, the right to ancestral power through the use of certain linguistic property such as sacred chants, and the right to manufacture certain ceremonial objects. Membership in these groups is permanent and public; the one fact that will be known about an Indian before anything else is his or her language group membership.
> (1977: 85; see also 1974: 74)

The language group is conceptualized by its members as agnates who trace descent from a set of ancestral founding brothers; the founding Eldest Brother is the focal ancestor of the entire group. Ancestral brothers are ranked according to seniority, as specified in the origin traditions of each sib. In this way, each language group is united in a comprehensive hierarchy.

The Sib

The Wanano list twenty-five sibs. Each is a named descent group whose members view themselves as descendants of one of the language group's founding ancestral brothers. The sib is the only social group in the Uaupés whose membership is conceptualized in terms of descent, rather than "siblingship." To the Wanano, it comprises "the grandchildren of one man" where "man" is a putative ancestor. Each Wanano sib possesses a unique repertoire of oral traditions relating to its founding ancestor and bears the name of that ancestor, plus the suffix -*pona*, meaning "children of." Genealogies are not maintained; rather, the naming system governs group membership.

The Local Group

There are ten Wanano settlements on the margin of the Uaupés River in Brazil.[3] Settlements contain up to 160 people and are located at least 3 km apart.

The Wanano conceive of the sib as a localized unit, established in its place by the ancestral anaconda canoe that placed the first ancestor of each sib in the "birthplace" of that sib.[4] However, the ideal of complete patrilocality is not fully realized and the degree of correspondence of the local group and the unilineal descent group varies. The local group is the only working unit in which membership can be acquired. Members can join, leave, and change locations. A settlement's residents frequently include client in-laws and other non-sib members.[5] Residents distinguish between *makari mahsa*, "belonging ones" who are sib members (or wives "marrying back"—see below), and *su ?sari mahsa*, "mixing ones," who are not. The *su ?sari masono* or "mixed one" is relegated to visitor status, regardless of whether the individual was born in the settlement.

Membership in a sib would appear to be automatic on the basis of patrilineal descent alone. Yet, in a jural sense, one is not a member of a sib until one receives the sib name. Only then does an individual become "alive" in the social sense.[6] Symbolically, the individual is given breath and life through the life-breath (*yeheripona*) of the sib ancestor whose name he or she bears. Through the name, the ancestor endows the recipient with the basic right to social existence and to a particular place and set of social, economic, and ritual privileges in the sib. The recipient, in turn, owes to the ancestor, and to the living sib, the obligation to live up to the name and all its attendant responsibilities.

This exchange process perpetuates sib life and determines the individual's rights and obligations. To a Wanano, the bearer of an ancestral name stands literally in exchange for that ancestor: Biari Ko?totaro is ancestor Biari's "exchange," his incarnation in the present. *Ko?totaro,* "the exchanged one," derives from the verb stem used to describe other kinds of exchange, such as sister exchange. Ancestor and descendant are linked in a reciprocal relationship: each endows the other with life. The ancestor's name breathes life into its recipient; at the same time, through this living incarnation, the ancestor retains a vital role in the society (Chernela 1982a).

Each sib controls a limited set of names that are its exclusive property and cannot be duplicated by members of any other sib. Within a sib, however, more than one person may bear the same name simultaneously. A first-born son takes the name of his paternal grandfather, who took the name of his paternal grandfather, and so forth. Later-born sons may take any of the names belonging to the grandfather's younger brothers. As siblings, ancestral and living, are always ranked according to seniority, so are the names. An invariant connotation of rank inheres in each name; name does not merely signify one's rank, it also validates it. Thus, a chief, the first-born of the first-born, receives a first-born name, and thereby claims his position in the hierarchy.

These beliefs and practices bear significantly on the social structure. By cycling ranked names through the generations, the exchange principle effectively eliminates time from the system and perpetuates the rank order. This social system replicates itself in every generation.

Local settlements often fragment. As groups grow in size, subgroups leave the original unit. The splinter group may establish its own settlement or may utilize bilateral kinship ties to reside in villages of relatives.

The sib, the name-owning group, rather than a lineage, constitutes the fundamental unit of Wanano society. The extreme value placed on sib unity becomes apparent when a sib breaks into unofficial, *de facto* segments. In such cases, as when a local sib splits, the bud group is denied a new identity. The phrase used to describe the sib, which translates as "one man's grandchildren," might logically be applied to a smaller unit; however, the term is considered absolutely inappropriate in reference to units below the sib level, and to use it in this way is offensive and antisocial. For the Wanano, sib subsegments are undesirable caucuses, arising only in hard times and threatening group unity. They are without legitimacy. Even if the Wanano could recall an ancestor three or five generations before, it would be considered inappropriate to divide the group by virtue of such a principle.

Rank

Rank positions are ascribed according to the principle of seniority by birth order. An individual's rank depends on the ancestor from whom his or her father descended. The sib ancestors are brothers ranked according to the order of their emergence from the ancestral anaconda canoe. At the level of the sib, all the descendants of a first-born ancestral brother are of higher rank than the descendants of a second-born ancestral brother, the latter descendants of higher rank than the descendants of a third-born ancestral brother, and so on, accounting for the relative ranked placements of all twenty-five sibs. This system is found in numerous societies throughout the world and has been termed the "conical clan" by Paul Kirchoff (1955).

Rank is a language of status, a language of relations among kin groups. In such a system, brotherhood and fatherhood are terms of group distinctions. Within a sib, all children of a higher-ranked man are senior to the children of a lesser-ranked man,[7] producing a rank order within the sib. The logic which an individual uses to calculate rank is simple: if my father called his (the addressee's) father "older brother," then I call him "older brother," regardless of his age. Only for children of one man does chronological age determine seniority. Thus, while the association between age and rank is literal for actual siblings, it is otherwise metaphoric.

Rank and Placement

As a form of social placement, rank is one aspect of the more comprehensive Wanano concept of placement—*duhisina*—which may be glossed as both "being" and "sitting." Its scope is tripartite, combining social, spatial, and temporal aspects. Each of the three parts of the construct is seen as a transformation of the others. This is the essence of Wanano conceptualization (see chapter 6).

The point is well illustrated by the following example, cited by the linguist Carolyn Waltz:

> The root *wa-* as in *wa?mi* "older brother" not only carries the meaning of rank, but also means "first." The same root is used in the word *wa?manore*, "a long time ago," or "in the beginning times," and also in the word *wa?ma* meaning "new." All through

the Guanano language, time and space are fused in various morphemes. This root carries with it the sense of rank and attaches
itself to anyone in the ranking line of the patrilineage.

On the other hand, the root *ba?* as in *ba?u,* "younger brother,"
denotes familiarity rather than the rank of respect for older
brother. Clues to the meaning of this morpheme are found in
Guanano vocabulary. It is used in such words as *ba?aro,* "later,"
and *ba?aro se?e,* "back side." This morpheme denotes younger
in time or lower in rank, and behind in space, again merging time
and space. (1980: 14–15)

This linguistic cojoining of temporal and spatial concepts reinforces the basic perspectives of structure, flexibility, and continuity.
Thus, while one will both sit "first" and descend from one who
came "first," those coming "later" will find identity from both being
"later" and "back."

Rank and Behavior

Rank is both precise and general. It denotes, in precise terms, the
unique location of every individual in relation to every other.
Within a sib, members of the highest-ranked line are referred to as
eldest brothers, Wamisima; the same term is used to refer to the five
highest sibs. The senior member of the sib—called "people's oldest
brother,"—*mahsa wami*—has chiefly prerogatives and obligations,
and represents the sib as its head to all other groups.[8] Rank plays an
important role in ritual performance, where many roles are assumed
according to rank.

Within the sib, the bond of common descent prevails; apart from
the distinctiveness of the primogeniture line, rank has minimal bearing on social interactions outside of the ritual context. In day-to-day
relations among different sibs, on the other hand, rank becomes a
determinant in personal identification and group interaction.

Sibs are grouped into ranked and named sociocentric classes to
which role terms are applied.[9] The classes are paired and linked by
a system of complementary "roles." Individuals of different rank
classes may use an alternate set of metaphoric kinship terms that
emphasizes genealogical distance and rank difference.

Kinship Metaphor: Generational Classes

In addition to the agnatic kin terminology used among individuals
and groups within the same language group, there is a second system

Table 2. *Reciprocal Generational Terms*

Generational class of speaker	Class of Addressee		
	Grandchild	Uncle	Grandparent
Grandchild	brother	uncle	grandparent
Uncle	nephew	brother	uncle
Grandparent	grandchild	nephew	brother

of classification that utilizes generational nomenclature to indicate hierarchical distance. This might be thought of as a system of generational classes.

Within the descent group, this classificatory scheme also ties into a system of reference and address in which five generational terms are applied reciprocally across the three levels, as shown in table 2 (for convenience only masculine forms are given).

Generational class terminology is used in two ways. On the one hand, it serves as a classificatory scheme in which all the sibs of a language group are classified into the ranked groupings "grandchildren," "uncles," and "grandparents." Contrary to what might be expected, grandchildren hold the highest rank, uncles are in the middle, and grandparents fall at the bottom of the scale. According to this scheme, every sib in the area has an absolute status, so that any other sib might say, for example, "They are grandfathers."

The concept of generational class structures relationships both within and among language groups. Within a language group, generational class relations are based on dominance and subordination. Among language groups, they are based upon equivalence. Within the language group, the concept of generational class can structure a range of behaviors and expectations, both economic and symbolic, as the cases presented below show.

Sib Hierarchy and Pairing

The twenty-five sibs are arranged in order: the first ten sibs are known collectively as the Wamisima, literally, "older brothers." Sibs eleven to fifteen (possibly with additional sibs in Colombia) are collectively termed Tibahana, "younger brothers." The remaining sibs, sixteen through twenty-five, are known as Wiroa, meaning "the perching bird" (family Pipridae), and are referred to as "servants." The Wamisima are classified as "chiefs" or "grandchildren";

the Tibahana as "uncles"; and the Wiroa as "slaves" or "grand-parents."

The descendants of the first of the twenty-five ancestral brothers are called "our oldest brothers" by the other sibs. Living descendants of the youngest ancestral brothers have the lowest rank and are referred to as "younger brothers." The Wamisima and Tibahana, whose origins are said to go back to the ancestral anaconda, are associated with the head and tail, respectively. These associations refer to the sequence and location of emergence from the mythical anaconda. A distinct origin is attributed to the Wiroa, who are said to have been created from perching birds by a powerful Wanano shaman.

A Case of Class Pairing in Practice

In Yapima (the site of my research), the sibs belong to the Wamisima (older brothers), while Wiroa sibs live in the nearby associated village of Soma. By virtue of ancestral precedent, both groups designate the Yapima sibs as "chiefly" and the Soma sibs as "servants." Buoyero, the founding eldest brother of the Wiroa, is said to have been the servant of Mukuti Yairo, the founding eldest brother of the Wamisima. Yapima residents address Soma residents as "grandpa" regardless of particular sib or relative age. (The equivalent for "grandpa" as a term of address conveys familiarity and is not the same as the equivalent for "grandfather," which is a term of respect.) Soma residents, correspondingly, address Yapima residents as "grandchildren."

Until recently, the Wiroa of Soma resided in Yapima and, according to informants of both chiefly and servant groups, performed services such as agricultural labor and house construction for the chiefly sibs. This labor continues, although the Wiroa now live in a nearby but separate settlement.

Marriage

The incest regulation forbids marrying or having sexual relations with anyone in one's own language group or phratry (brother group) and, conversely, requires that one marry into a different language and kin group. This is the basic rule on which the marriage system is founded. From the perspective of the Wanano and all other members of their multilanguage phratry, the world in this way divides into two parts: "brothers" and "marriageables." Each sib maintains ongoing marital alliances with several other sibs in the large field of marriageables.

Two strongly stated preferences govern marriage practices: sister exchange and marriage with a patrilateral cross-cousin.

Sister Exchange

Marriages are considered to be exchanges between sibs and are arranged by the sib seniors. When a simultaneous exchange of women occurs, the marriage is called *koto tarikoro*, "woman exchange." When the negotiation is not immediately reciprocal, it is called *pubuhseri manenikoro*, "no woman given in exchange," indicating that the debt is outstanding until a return is made. During my stay in Yapima in 1978, a woman whose daughter had married four years earlier complained because no return had yet been made, and her 18-year-old son was wifeless. A claim is made when a wife is needed; otherwise, a debt may remain outstanding for many years. In this case the debt was repaid when a female became eligible in 1981, three years after the claim was issued. Once the exchange is reciprocated, the term implying indebtedness is no longer used.

Preferred Marriage to Patrilateral Cross-Cousin

There is a strongly stated preference for a son to marry his father's sister's daughter. Ideally, this would be the father's actual sister's daughter or the daughter of one of the father's classificatory sisters, who is a member of the father's own sib. Less ideally, the bride may be a daughter of any Wanano female the father calls "sister," that is, of any Wanano woman of his own generation. Having married, these Wanano women no longer live in the sib settlement.

Marriage with a matrilateral cross-cousin is also permitted, although it is less preferred than marriage to a father's sister's daughter. The rule is that spouses be taken only from among father's sisters' children and mother's brothers' children, who constitute the cross-cousin category, or *tanyü/o*.[10]

Father's-sister's-daughter marriage is considered the most correct form of marriage. In this case a woman marries into her mother's sib and is said to be "marrying back." A woman who marries back is a "belonging woman," *makari koro*. Wives who have "married back" are distinguished from wives who have married into villages where they have no mother's brothers and are placed in the category of "mixers" (see chapter 6).

Ongoing Affinity

Patrilateral cross-cousin marriage carries with it no obligation or compulsion to perpetuate exchange (Lévi-Strauss 1969), for each direct marital exchange, once balanced, may be considered final. The Wanano combine this "discontinuous exchange" with a preference for marriage into the sib in which the sib ancestor married. Thus, Wanano patrilateral exchange offers flexibility in marriage choice, on the one hand, and a preference for continuity, on the other.

Marriage alliances among sibs are considered to have been established by the ancestors. Thus, the Wanano sib Biari Pona (descendants of Biari) say that Biari's wife belonged to the Desana sib Simi Paro Pona; therefore, their wives must all be from that sib. The Biari Pona have adhered to that rule, eventually inviting the affinal sib to reside with them. These two sibs live together and marry each other, as would be expected in a case of classical dual organization (see chapter 10). This example of sib exogamy without local exogamy is a departure from the usual Wanano pattern. This is a unique ethnographic case of exogamous moieties speaking different languages at the same location.

More commonly, sibs maintain marriage alliances with several sibs simultaneously, and marriages even occur where ongoing affinity has not been established.

Multiple Marriage Alliances: The Wekbea and Yahuri Cases

Sibs that maintain ongoing marital ties with more than one sib attribute this practice to ongoing affinity and ancestral precedence. One member of the Diani Pona told me, "Diani married a Desana, but his brothers married Baniwa women."

The village in which I was based consisted of two high-ranking sibs: the Wekbea and Yahuri sibs. Of a total of eight marriages in this settlement, all but two men had taken as first wife their father's sister's daughter (at the sib level—i.e., the daughter of a woman from ego's own sib).[11] However, these wives came from six different sibs, all of which maintain ongoing affinity with the Wekbea and Yahuri. In the exceptional cases, one married a father's sister's daughter of greater kinship distance (i.e., her mother, although Wanano, was not from the husband's sib), and the other married his mother's brother's daughter. One 23-year-old Yahuri man married a 40-year-old father's sister's daughter: the discrepancy in age was less important than the suitability of category.

Variation: The Wiroa Example

High-ranking groups such as the Wekbea and Yahuri carefully distinguish between *"real* in-laws" and "in-laws," using the emphatic affix for the first. Whereas the Biari, Wekbea, and Yahuri had almost all taken wives who were daughters of sib "sisters," the Wiroa had taken wives from a broader range of sibs, cousins of far greater distance.

Generational Class, Rank, and Marriage

The Wanano at Yapima hold that marriage may take place only between status equals. Status equals are knowable because, as we have seen, the internal structures of the language groups are identical. Each is composed of sibs ranked from first to last and classified according to generational class. Once the sib of a person is known, the parameters of relation follow.

Marriage is sanctioned only between sibs belonging to different language groups who are of the same generational class. Thus, the grandchild/chiefly sibs of language group A exchange wives with the grandchild/chiefly sibs of language groups B, C, and so forth.

As noted, kin terms can be used only between members of "brother" groups (i.e., those belonging to the same generational class). Thus, a prospective husband considers the daughter of a parent's cross-sibling to be a mother's brother's daughter (MBD)[12] or father's sister's daughter (FZD)—and hence marriageable—only if she is a member of a sib of the same generational class as ego's mother (and thus ego himself, assuming that his father married appropriately). If she is of a different generational class, she is not referred to as a cross-cousin, but rather by the generational class term that applies to her sib. I have heard young people chastised for flirting with inappropriate partners and told that the objects of their intentions were not "cross-cousins"—although by straightforward genealogical reckoning they are indeed cross-cousins—but "uncles," "aunts," or "grandparents."

The variation in marriage practices between people of different ranks suggests an interesting pattern. The highest-ranked sibs adhere most closely to the rules, saying that to violate them would disrupt the terminological system: "It would create chaos" and "You would not know what to call anyone." In high-ranking groups, those who depart from the norm are subject to ostracism. In Yapima, one married woman was not a FZD to her husband. She was a MBD, daughter of the brother of a second wife, and a person of lower rank. Because of this lower rank, concern was expressed that her children were "bad" (*nya*, same gloss as "ugly") and no one would want to marry them. The pejorative epithet here, like the pejorative relational substitute for cross-cousin above, is a choice that is both political and personal.

Arranging marriages often entails a trade-off between immediacy of need and correctness of relation. Marriageable females are said to be scarce due to the restrictive preference for marriage with first cross-cousins. Single men lament this dilemma in the following song:

> Isn't it strange?
> I have no cousins;
> I am alone and I haven't any cousin.
> Fortunately for me,
> I have fathers of my fathers;
> But I have no cousin.[13]

The highest-ranked sibs insist upon maintaining the preferred pattern at the expense of expediency. In this way they consolidate their alliances; to deviate from them would be to admit spouses of unequal rank, thus disrupting the social order. Lower-ranked sibs place fewer restrictions on marriage choices, permitting marriage to females other than closely related mother's brother's and father's sister's daughters.

Commonly, sibs maintain ongoing alliances with several sibs simultaneously. Each alliance is based upon principles of direct exchange, yet more than two groups are involved. Furthermore, each of the in-law sibs maintains its own alliances, each of which is based on principles of restricted exchange.

The highest-ranked Wanano sib, the Biari Pona, practiced restricted exchange, maintaining an ongoing marriage alliance with a single in-law sib (see chapter 10). Men of the Wekbea and Yahuri (second- and third-ranked sibs, respectively) married close kin within the preferred *tanyü* and *tanyo* cross-cousin categories, exclusively.

The low-ranking Wiroa attach less importance to the rule of father's sister's daughter marriage. Their choices appear to be subject to a wider range of factors, including expediency. This suggests that they do not subscribe to the same model as do the high-ranked groups.

Summary

Uaupés social structure may be described as a system of exogamous and hierarchically ordered descent groups, which are intersected by intermarrying, horizontal status classes, here termed "generational classes." Relations within the descent group are governed by kinship and characterized by dominance and subordination; relations among descent groups are governed by marriage (actual or potential), which normally takes place between status equals.

In the Uaupés, concepts of siblingship and seniority supersede true descent—with significant structural consequences. The metaphor of siblingship unites agnatic groups at every level; seniority differentiates them, so that every individual within a sib, and every sib within a language group, stands in a fixed rank relationship to every other. The exchange of names replicates the order of seniority in each succeeding generation.

The concept of generational class describes yet another relationship. Like siblingship, generational class is couched in the language of kinship; but, unlike siblingship, it does not denote actual kin relations. As the distinction between older and younger brothers ranks individuals and groups in the descent system, so does the opposition "grandfather"/"grandchild" mark relative status in the generational class system (although the younger term signifies superiority in this system). Most significantly, the generational class system structures relationships among groups. Within the language group, the concept of generational class unites the highest- and lowest-rank sibs into an ongoing relationship represented as dominance/subordination involving the exchange of resources for service. Across language groups, sibs of the same generational class status are paired, as equals, in a continually renewed relationship based upon the exchange of women.

Chapter 5. Kinship Nomenclature

WANANO KIN TERMINOLOGY IS OF THE cross-cousin or two-line type (Dole 1991),[1] a pattern found with frequency in all parts of the world. Wanano of the same generation address and refer to one another as siblings. Those in ego's sibling category include the children of father's actual brothers, as well as the children of all Wanano males of father's generation. This system of kin classification does not segregate cousins of differing degrees of collaterality to ego. Rather, criteria of collaterality in ego's generation are subordinate to other factors.

A primary organizing principle of the same system, instead, is the discrimination of relatives linked through father from those linked through mother. Whereas own-generation speakers of father's language are categorized as siblings, own-generation speakers of mother's language are classified as "in-laws," regardless of degrees of distance from mother or father. The social universe is thus divided into two major categories of persons, "our people," comprised of lineal and parallel kin, and cross-relatives, who are "others." For participants in such a system, kin proximity is a factor of descent group membership rather than the genealogical distance between individuals.

Wanano kinship nomenclature shares many general features with terminological systems recorded elsewhere in the Uaupés (see tables 3, 4, 5), but at the same time presents significant variations. The kinship terms analyzed in this chapter are used both in address and reference unless otherwise indicated. The kin terms are obligatorily preceded by one of the following possessive pronouns: *yü-* (my), *mü-* (your), or *to-* (his or hers). The gender morphemes *-ü*, denoting male referent, and *-o*, denoting female referent, are affixed to the stem.

As elsewhere in the Uaupés, each generation has a separate set of terms. For the grandparent ($+2$) and grandchild (-2) generations, only two terms are used: *nüchü* (masc.) and *nücho* (fem.) for grand-

Table 3. *Comparison of Kinship Terminology for Relatives of Second Ascending and Descending Generations*

| | | | Language | | |
	Wanano	Cubeo	Bará	Barasana	Makuna
FF, MF	nüchü	nyekú	ñihku	nīkü	ñikü
FM, MM	nücho	nyéko	ñihkó	nīko	ñiko
ZS, DS	panami	panaíhinkü	párami	hanami	hanami
ZD, DD	panamaio	panaíhinko	párameo	hanenyo	haneño
Source	Author	(Goldman 1963:126, 134)	(Jackson 1977:89)	(C. Hugh-Jones 1979:79)	(Århem, 1981:37)

Note: I have followed the orthographic conventions of the author cited.

Table 4. *Comparison of Kinship Terminology for Male Agnates of First Ascending Generation*

| | | | Language | | |
	Wanano	Cubeo	Bará	Barasana	Makuna
FB		baküdyo	bügü	büamü	büamü
FOB	pükami				
FYB	pükübü				
Source	Author	(Goldman 1963:134)	(Jackson 1977:89)	(C. Hugh-Jones 1979:79, fig. 10)	(Århem 1981:37)

Table 5. *Comparison of Zero Generation Kin Terms*

| | | | Language | | |
	Wanano	Cubeo	Bará	Barasana	Makuna
OB, OZ	wami(-o)	himámikü/o	hwü/hō	gagü/o	bai(iño)
YB, YZ	bü?ü (ba?o)	híyokü/o	baü/bayó	bedi (bedeo)	kien(omí)
Source	Author	(Goldman 1963:34)	(Jackson 1983:112)	(C. Hugh-Jones 1979:78)	(Århem 1981:37)

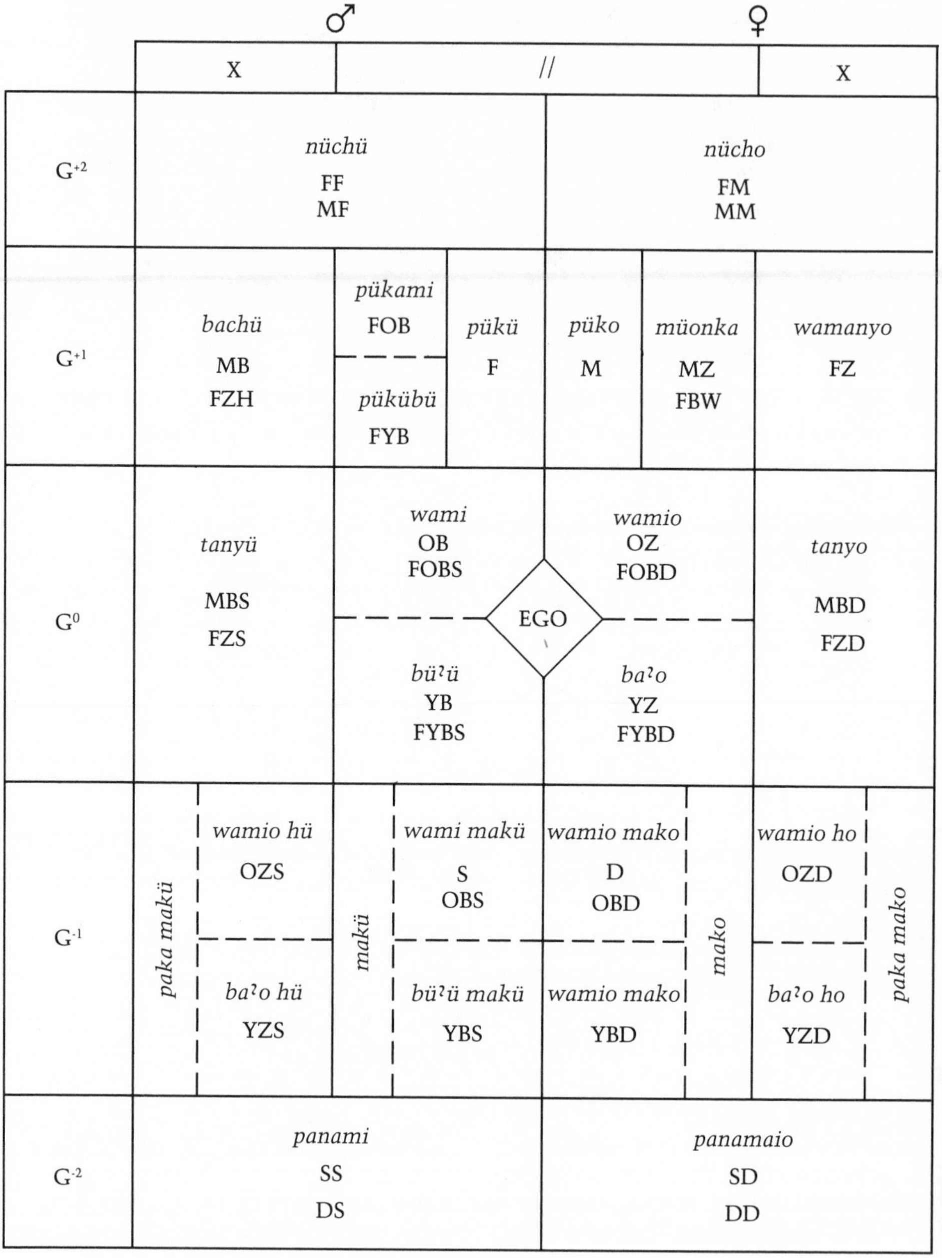

	♂ X	//			♀ X
G^{+2}	*nüchü* FF MF				*nücho* FM MM
G^{+1}	*bachü* MB FZH	*pükami* FOB / *pükübü* FYB	*pükü* F	*püko* M | *müonka* MZ FBW	*wamanyo* FZ
G^{0}	*tanyü* MBS FZS	*wami* OB FOBS / *büʔü* YB FYBS	EGO	*wamio* OZ FOBD / *baʔo* YZ FYBD	*tanyo* MBD FZD
G^{-1}	*paka makü*	*wamio hü* OZS / *baʔo hü* YZS	*makü* | *wami makü* S OBS / *büʔü makü* YBS	*wamio mako* D OBD / *wamio mako* YBD | *mako*	*wamio ho* OZD / *baʔo ho* YZD | *paka mako*
G^{-2}	*panami* SS DS				*panamaio* SD DD

Figure 3. Paradigm of Wanano kinship nomenclature (simplified).

parent and *panami* (masc.) and *panamaio* (fem.) for grandchild. These terms express only the sex and the generation of the referent. For these two generations, no distinction is made between mother's and father's relatives. The Wanano terms closely resemble Cubeo, Bará, Barasana, and Makuna terms for the same relatives (see table 3).

The pattern of terms for the first ascending (parental), first descending (offspring), and ego generations differs from the pattern of the second ascending and descending generations in that father's relatives are distinguished from mother's, separating one's own patrilineal kin group from mother's relatives (fig. 3). I treat these terms as two separate classes in accordance with the Wanano distinction of own kin, which I here call "agnatic," and other's, which I call "affinal," for reasons described below.

Agnatic Relatives

Agnates of the First Ascending Generation

The term for father is *pükü*, composed of the morphemes *pük-*, denoting + 1 generation, and the gender suffix *-ü*, denoting masculine referent. Father's sister is also denoted by a single term—*wamanyo*—which is used for all female Wanano of first ascending generation.

Terms for father's siblings extend to persons of father's generation throughout the language group and are also used for members of different language groups within the same phratry. Terms for father's brothers contain the morpheme *pük-*, denoting + 1 generation for own kin, combined with a morpheme denoting sibling order. The term *pükübü* is used for father's younger brother as well as for any Wanano male of lower rank than father in father's generation. The term *pükami* is used for father's older brother as well as for any Wanano male of higher rank than father in father's generation. In distinguishing these relatives from one another by rank (see tables 4 and 5 and fig. 4), the Wanano terms for male agnates in the first ascending generation differ in an interesting way from those reported for other Uaupés groups such as the Cubeo (Goldman 1963), Bará (Jackson 1977, 1983), Barasana (C. Hugh-Jones 1979; S. Hugh-Jones 1979), and Makuna (Århem 1981).

Agnates of the Zero Generation

The classification of agnates according to rank in the zero generation is well established in the literature on the Uaupés groups. For

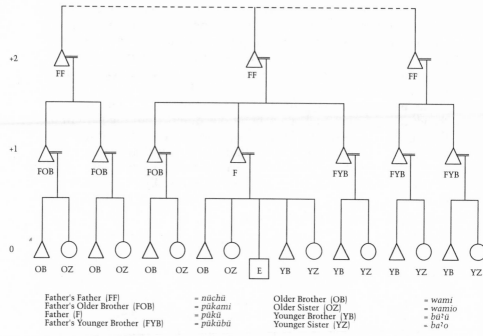

Father's Father (FF)	= *nüchü*	Older Brother (OB)	= *wami*
Father's Older Brother (FOB)	= *pükami*	Older Sister (OZ)	= *wamio*
Father (F)	= *pükü*	Younger Brother (YB)	= *büʔü*
Father's Younger Brother (FYB)	= *pükübü*	Younger Sister (YZ)	= *baʔo*

Figure 4. Wanano agnatic terminology showing rank indicators for first ascending and zero generations (this terminology extends to all Wanano and to all members of phratric groups).

the Wanano, *wami* and *büʔü* refer to older and younger brother, respectively, and *wamio* and *baʔo* to older and younger sister, respectively. This is a general pattern in the Uaupés, as can be seen in table 5. It will be recalled that "older" and "younger" are not indicators of age, but of relative rank.

Agnates of the First Descending Generation

A male classes his own offspring and the offspring of all kin in his generation as *makü* (masc.) and *mako* (fem.). These terms may be glossed as "son" and "daughter" and are only applied to the children of one's own kin group. In Dakota-Iroquois-Dravidian groups, sister's son and daughter (male speaking) are always distinguished terminologically from own (and brother's) son and daughter. Sisters' sons or daughters are not of ego's own descent group; from the Wanano point of view they are affinal relatives, and terms for them are discussed under affines.

Another feature of Wanano terminology not reflected in reports on other Uaupés societies is that through combinations of basic terms relatives in the first descending generation may also be distinguished according to the rank of linking relatives. These compound terms are used more to mark superior-ranked siblings' sons or daughters than to mark the sons or daughters of a sibling of lesser rank.

OBS	*wami makü*
OBD	*wami mako*
YBS	*büʔü makü*
YBD	*büʔü mako*

Similar compound terms can distinguish the children of "older" and "younger" sisters, but these children are not agnatic kin (see below).

The use of suffixes further emphasizes rank: the morphemes *-suma* (masc.) and *-sanumia* (fem.), and *-na* (masc.) and *-nanumia* (fem.) are status indicators affixed to agnatic terms to stress the rank of the referent (Waltz and Waltz 1980: 4). The first set is honorific, stressing the referent's higher rank; the second set emphasizes the referent's lower rank.

A woman refers to her brothers' children as *papükü* (masc.) and *papüko* (fem.), regardless of rank. These are members of her own kin group, which, as noted, may be extended to the entire language group. These nephews and nieces are the preferred marriage partners for female ego's own children.

Affinal Relatives

The term for mother is *püko*, derived from *pük-*, a morpheme denoting +1 generation, and *-o*, the gender morpheme denoting female. From a sociocentric point of view, mother is an affine for the Wanano in that she is member of a group that is affinal to ego's own. This separation is not borne out lexically, however: the term for mother differs from the term for father by only a gender marker.

A man refers to his own wife with the term *namo*. He refers to the wives of fellow Wanano of his generation (his classificatory brothers) as *buhibuo*. If, however, he wishes to stress the linking brother's rank, he can use the expressions *wami namo* or *büʔü namo*, which point to relative status. A woman uses the term *nasamo* in referring to her brothers' wives. She uses *manu* to refer to husband.

Table 6. Wanano Zero Generational Terminology

Agnatic	Affinal	"Mother's Children"	"Father's Sister's Children"
wami (OB)	tanyo (FZD, MBD)	püko makü/o (MZS and MZD when MZH ≠ FB)	wamanyo makü/o (FZS and FZD when FZH ≠ MB)
wamio (OZ)	tanyü (FZS, MBS)		
bü?ü (YB)			
ba?o (YZ)			

Table 7. Wanano Terms outside the Expected Pattern for Two-Line Alliance Structure

Generation	Wanano Term	English Gloss
+1	püko manu	mother's husband
0	püko makü/o	mother's children
	wamanyo makü/o	father's sister's children
−1	namo makü/o	wife's children

Affines of the First Ascending Generation

The incest regulation forbids marriage (and sexual relations) with anyone in one's own language group and, conversely, requires that one marry into a different language and kin group. This is the basic rule on which the marriage system is founded.

Marriage occurs within one's own generation. Relatives of the sibling category (i.e., wami/o, "older" brother and "older" sister, bü?ü/ba?o, "younger" brother and "younger" sister) are forbidden as marriage partners. The ideal is to marry one's own father's sister's child or mother's brother's child. This preferred marriage partner is called tanyü (masc.) or tanyo (fem.). (I know of a woman who left her husband after a single day of marriage, claiming that it was neither binding nor legitimate because, as she said to him, "I am not your tanyo.")

The strong preference for marriage to a cross-cousin is combined with a norm of sister exchange. Wanano nomenclature reflects this system of restricted, symmetrical exchange by denoting both mother's brother and father's sister's husband with the single term bachü. Similarly, there is a single term for mother's sister and for father's

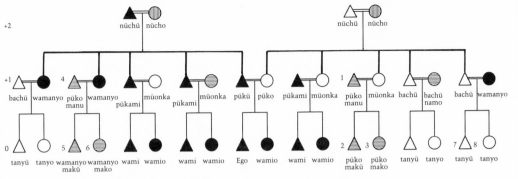

Figure 5a. +2, +1, and 0 generation kin terms, showing departure from two-line terminological system.

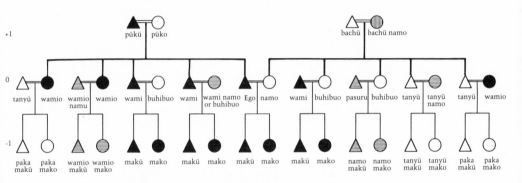

Figure 5b. +1, 0, and −1 generation kin terms for male speaker (Ego), showing departure from two-line terminological system.

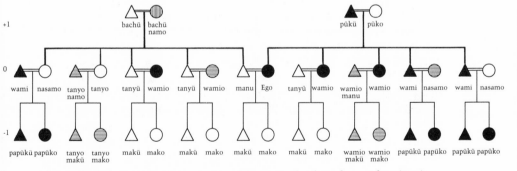

Figure 5c. +1, 0, and −1 generation kin terms for female speaker (Ego), showing departure from two-line terminological system.

Solid symbols indicate Wanano individuals (or members of any of the Wanano phratric groups); open symbols indicate members of ego's mother's group; symbols with horizontal fill indicate individuals who are neither Wanano nor from mother's group. When the group affiliation of an individual does not affect terminology, the fill is vertical. Rank and age distinctions are generally omitted. Where necessary, the term for elder or most senior is used. All diagrams present kinship terminology relative to the individual labeled ego.

brother's wife: *müonka*. With ongoing sister exchange, these relatives would be ego's parents-in-law. Accordingly, these terms signify
parents-in-law as well as genealogical relatives.

Kinship nomenclature does provide for divergence from the preferred pattern (see tables 6 and 7 and fig. 5). For example, when father's sister's husband is not from mother's group, and therefore not a
classificatory mother's brother, he is called *püko manu*, a compound term that may be glossed as "mother's husband." This distinguishes him from *bachü*, the category of father-in-law, and places
his children outside of the preferred category of potential affines.

The same term is used for mother's sister's husband if he is not a
Wanano (i.e., classificatory father's brother). If the practice of restricted exchange were strictly maintained, mother's sister's husband would be father's own or classificatory brother. The Wanano
system of nomenclature in this way diverges from a rigorous divi-
sion of one's relatives into agnates and affines, for affines may be
subdivided into "in-laws," with whom ongoing marriage alliances
are perpetuated, and "in-laws of in-laws," who fall outside of ego's
ongoing alliances.

Affines of the Zero Generation

As we have seen, all Wanano in ego's own generation are classified
as siblings. Cross-cousins (i.e., FZS/D and MBS/D), are called *tanyü*
for males and *tanyo* for females, a cousin pattern known as Iroquois.
This follows from the fact that all (and only) siblings and parallel
cousins are Wanano, and cross-cousins are not Wanano. It is from
the *tanyü/o* category that ego must take a marriage partner.

When mother's sister's husband is not a Wanano, mother's sister's
children are referred to as *püko makü* (masc.) or *püko maco* (fem.),
literally, "mother's children." These would be ego's classificatory
siblings were there strict dual organization. Likewise, when father's
sister's husband is not from mother's group, her children are called
wamanyo makü/o, literally, "father's sister's children." The terms
püko makü/o and *wamanyo makü/o* distinguish these relatives
from either the classificatory "sibling" (kin) class or the marriageable cousin class.

Affines of the First Descending Generation

Sister's children are potential spouses to a man's own children and
are distinguished from brother's children, who are kin. This cross-
nephew or niece is the preferred marriage partner for a male ego's

own child. For a man, sister's son and sister's daughter are *paka makü* and *paka mako*, respectively. These terms may also be applied to the children of all Wanano females of ego's generation. Two alternate terms designating sister's children emphasize the relative rank of the sister—*wamiohü/o* and *ba?ohü/o* refer to "older" sister's son or daughter and "younger" sister's son or daughter, respectively.

A male refers to all Wanano of first descending generation as *makü* or *mako*, or *wami makü/o* or *bü?ü makü/o* for higher-rank sibling's children and lower-rank sibling's children, respectively. These parallel nephews and nieces are prohibited as marriage partners for ego's children. In contrast, *paka makü/o* or, alternatively, *wamiohü* and *ba?ohü*—distinguishing "older" (i.e., higher-ranked) sibling's children from "younger" (i.e., lower-ranked) sibling's children—are the terms used for cross-nephews and nieces. These are the preferred marriage partners for ego's own children.

When the rules of restricted exchange are followed, son's wife will be male ego's *paka mako* and female ego's *papüko*. *Makü namono* is yet another compound expression, in this case meaning "son's wife," which is applied when the marriage rule is not followed and son's wife is not *paka mako*.

When wife's sister has married a man who is not one's classificatory brother, her son and daughter are called *namo makü/o*, meaning "wife's children," placing them outside the restricted pattern.

Discussion

Cross-cousin systems characteristically distinguish kin from affines terminologically. The Wanano, like the other Uaupés groups, the Bará, Barasana, and Makuna, deviate from the standard pattern of dual opposition of cross and parallel relatives.

The possibility of combining terms indicates flexibility in the terminological system that reflects variation in marriage practice. Nomenclature that accommodates variation appears to be more extensive than has been shown for the Bará, Barasana, and Makuna cases, where they are reported for only matrilateral kin of the zero generation. For example, *püko manu* (made up of terms for mother and husband) is the term of reference for father's sister's husband when he is not (classificatory or real) mother's brother, and for mother's sister's husband when he is not Wanano. In the zero generation, the terms *püko makü* and *püko mako* (compound terms that literally mean mother's child) are used for son and daughter of mother's sister when mother's sister's husband is not father's brother. The terms *wamanyo makü* and *wamanyo mako* are used for father's sister's children when father's sister is not married to a man from ego's own mother's group. Furthermore, the compound terms *tanyü/o makü/o,* for the children of cross-cousins, demonstrate yet another variation on two-line restricted exchange.

When two groups practice cross-cousin marriage with sister exchange over generations, the man marked in the diagram (fig. 5a) as #1 would necessarily be a member of ego's own group (real or classificatory FB). It would follow, then, that his children (#2, #3) would be ego's classificatory siblings and therefore not marriageable. When man #1 is not Wanano, his children, the cousins numbered here as #2 and #3, are neither "kin" nor "affine," but *püko makü/o,* "mother's children." Conversely, given sister exchange, male #4 would be a member of mother's group (classificatory or real MB). If he were from mother's own group, he would be called *bachü,* ego's potential father-in-law. If he is not mother's brother, he is referred to as *püko manu,* mother's husband, and his children (#5 and #6) called *wamanyo makü* and *wamanyo mako* (FZS and FZD). If he had been from mother's group, his children would have been called by the marriageable cross-cousin terms *tanyü/o.*

The solid figures in ego's generation are classified as siblings. The hatched figures are classified as siblings if the numbered parent is Wanano. If he is not, these relatives are not restricted by incest taboo, nor are they preferred. The only preferred marriage is with father's sister's children or mother's brother's children, of the categories *tanyü* and *tanyo.*

Jackson (1972, 1977) has drawn attention to a third set of terms in ego's generation. Jackson glosses *pahko-mahkü* and *pahko-mahko* as male and female matrilateral parallel cousins (1977: 89–90). This would not be appropriate for the Wanano, for as I have pointed out, mother's sister is, in the ideal and often in fact, married to father's brother. When mother's sister is married to father's brother (or any Wanano), their children will be Wanano and ego's classificatory siblings. Only when mother's sister is not married to a classificatory father's brother are her children *püko makü/o* (mother's children)—neither "siblings" nor marriageables. I am presenting a fourth category of zero generation terms and additional terms for first ascending and descending generations, indicating new examples of terms that express variation from the presumed ideal two-line terminological system.

For Jackson, the third cousin category forms a "third group." For the Wanano, the terms for mother's children, like *wamanyo makü/o,* and the other terms mentioned above for the +1 and −1 generations denote those specifically without a group designation—that is, neither kin nor marriageables from ego's point of view. These persons are considered "other," *paye masono*. Having no place in the scheme of proper two-part cross-cousin organization, they are placed outside of it and are designated by terms that from ego's viewpoint virtually negate kin proximity and group affiliation.

The terms referred to as "in-laws of in-laws" are never more than a set of terms. The persons designated by these terms are not integrated into either a formal or sociological unity. Rather than weakening the basic dualistic structure, they seem to reinforce it by naming variations and rendering them nonreproducible and, hence, without structural continuity.

Summary

In summary, the Uaupés system of classification is such that every other Uaupés individual may be referred to as a relative or an in-law. Its potential for both inclusiveness and exclusiveness is strong, as is characteristic of Uaupés social life in general. Its major features are: (1) segregation of patrilineal relatives; (2) use of relative age and generational metaphors to express rank; and (3) an equation between the cross-cousin and "in-law" categories.

Chapter 6. Gender, Language, and Placement in Wanano Poetic Forms

FOR THE WANANO AND OTHER Eastern Tukanoans, language is not only a symbol matrix; it is itself a symbol, a marker of identity and a primary definer of category. Speech is used to distinguish humans, who speak human languages, from nonhumans, who are thought to speak their own languages. The fundamental feature of boundary maintenance for most groups is linguistic distinctness.[1] Language is at once a manifestation of "natural" kin ties and the most revered cultural artifact. Eloquent speech, manifest in numerous genres, is considered of great value.

Songs and Key Concepts

Wanano speech performances are a rich source of data from which to gain insight into Wanano systems of thought. The lyrics of Wanano song powerfully convey the notion of placement and its importance in that society. In this chapter, we will examine the content of secular songs and litanies to explore the Wanano conceptualization of the self and its elaboration in metaphors of placement. By this I mean not only an individual or group's location in space, although this is one aspect of the concept. The term refers as well to the location of the self in relation to others living in the society and in relation to those who have gone before.

I am specifically concerned with two terms that designate social category: *makariro*, "the belonging one," and *su?sari masono*, "the mixed one." These categories are discussed in relation to a third term, *duhisina*, "sitting-being." Through these concepts the Wanano fuse time and space.

Makariro refers to one who "sits" in his ancestor's place. In contrast, *su?sari masono* glosses as "mixed one," a wanderer who has no stopping place. A *su?sari masono* resides in a settlement outside his or her own sib; the term refers to long-term visitors or those born in villages where they are not sib members. The notion of belonging is related to a third term, *duhisina*, "sitting-being," morphologically related to *duhinia*, "the sitting place," a place in the sense of homestead or settlement. Proper placement or "seatedness" signifies well-being. Sitting-being, then, is the primary act for the Wanano. One who is properly seated may belong. In fact, only one who is properly seated can "speak with authority": thus, *duhtiriro* refers to "the seated" or "placed one" as well as the "commanding one." In short, proper sitting, and the implied sense of belonging, requires appropriate location in the physical world. In addition, sitting involves placement in time. Ideally, one sits in the place of one's ancestors; to link the generations is to be in one's place.

Gender and Language

Since rules prohibit marriage with a member of one's own language group, marriage links distinct language groups in in-law relation to one another. In such a system, monocommunication is viewed as self-oriented, isolated, and incestuous, while multicommunication is viewed as other-oriented, sociable, and contractual.

Because of the combined practices of linguistic exogamy and patrilocal residence, in-marrying women in a Uaupés settlement speak a different language than that spoken by their husbands and grown children. Linguistically, they are outsiders.

The difference is maintained for its structural role, rather than for any prestige that accrues to any one language over another. A person is simply expected to speak his or her father's language rather than his or her mother's language. Group members identify as a group through the father's language, militating against linguistic pluralism and accommodation by members.

Linguistic distinctions are maintained, even when speakers are competent in one another's languages. It is quite ordinary for two speakers to be engaged in a conversation in which each speaks his or her own language since both females and males are multilingual. Children learn the languages of both their mothers and fathers but are discouraged from speaking their mothers' languages as they mature. As adults, men and women speak the language of their fathers and thus of their descent group, but understand their mothers' languages perfectly. In the acquisition process, then, one language, father's, becomes standard and public; while another language, mother's, is nonstandard and private.

Although the Wanano conceive of the sib as a localized unit, established in its place by the ancestral anaconda canoe, the ideal of

complete patrilocality is not always realized. The local and the unilineal descent groups may correspond to varying degrees. When a
splinter group leaves a settlement it may establish a new homestead
or may exploit bilateral kinship ties to reside in villages of relatives.
Settlement relocation disrupts the correspondence between descent
and locality, dividing residents into *makariro* and *su?sari masono*—
the "belonger" and the "mixer."

The female's view of descent and locality is the inverse of the
male's. Because of linguistic exogamy and patrilocality, a woman is
wife and mother to members of a descent-language group that is not
her own, one that holds a different claim on her allegiance than on
theirs (Chernela 1988a, c). Women of the same language group tend
to form monolingual clusters of solidarity in a village, calling one
another by the term "sister" and speaking more often to one another
than to other wives. In the Wanano village of Yapima, where I resided, the eight in-marrying wives spoke five different languages.

A woman's marriage to her mother's brother's son reduces this
conflict to a greater extent than any other marriage choice, because
she is marrying into her mother's own descent group. The conflict
is further reduced if that marriage is part of a sister exchange between the two families. By marrying into her mother's sib, a woman
becomes a "belonging one."

Wanano Song Performance

Improvised songs constitute one exchange in a sequence of events
that together comprise the *po?oa*, an exchange ritual carried out
among local descent groups. As described in chapter 8, the central
event of the *po?oa* is the exchange of specialized food or craft gifts.
Additional forms of exchange occur throughout the course of ritual
events, forming a nested hierarchy of ritual exchanges within the
principal ritual, with each exchange constituting a different means
through which the social system is communicated and the social
contract is reaffirmed. Among the various modes of exchange is the
language exchange, of which the song exchange (Wanano *basa ko-
totaro*) is one part.

Sib seniors carry out the transfer of gifts in the center of the dance
house beginning with the early morning arrival of the donors. The
morning sequence of events takes place in the center of the house
in full view of an attentive company, seated along the house walls
surrounding the performance activity. At midday the gifts are transferred and placed behind an enclosure in the hosting sib's quarters.
At this time the afternoon song dialogues begin.

The song exchanges accompany beer exchanges in which hosts and guests offer one another beer, following elaborate rules. An individual dispensing beer moves along the row of spectators, seated according to rank, offering a gourd ladle of beer to each spectator in turn. A beer donor may initiate a song exchange with a recipient at any point. The recipient is expected to drink the full contents of the ladle and return it empty, with a song.

While the morning's ceremonies take place at the center of the house, afternoon performances occur along the house walls. The audience, orderly and attentive during the morning's rituals, in the afternoon bustles with movement and talk. Afternoon performances are centerless; they consist of two-part exchanges that may occur at any location on the periphery. The two-part exchanges of the afternoon assume no greater audience than the performers themselves. The simultaneous song exchanges in different parts of the hall contribute to the apparent "privacy" of the exchange. In fact, nearby listeners do overhear an exchange, and there is no doubt that a performer attempts to draw as wide an audience as possible.

The song constitutes part of a spontaneous dialogue, whose subject is the self. Through metaphoric imagery, each singer presents himself or herself to others, producing a continuous dialectic of objectification and identification. The songs excerpted below, performed during beer exchanges, were selected for their concern with issues of placement. They also reveal the personal experience of language as a primary source of identity in a multilingual setting.

Texts of Secular Songs

Song of a Belonging Male

The following song was performed by a man of the Yahuri Pona sib who is married to a Desana female. (All proper names in the following account have been changed.) The terms "older" and "younger," here and elsewhere, refer to rank seniority. His reference to the listener's "older," classificatory sister is a boastful reminder that his Desana wife is senior in rank to the Desana listener. His use of the term "Other" (*paye masüno*) emphasizes the difference in language group identities: the singer is Wanano; the "Other" Desana. Whenever "Other" is used it connotes distance and alienation.

We, yes, we, yes.
You, yes, you, yes,
Are Desana.

But you will never stand up to me.
You, Desana, are from a place in Colombia,
The "other" place.
But you will never touch me.
You will never be equal to a Yahuri Pona.
And, as the day dawns,
"I, yes,
Am a person accustomed to taking the calabash,"
Says the Yahuri Ponairo, that I am!
You, yes, you, yes,
Will never stand a Wanano Yahuri Pona man . . .
You can't tolerate me because
I'm someone used to taking the calabash . . .
I am your brother-in-law,
Brother-in-law, Desana, who has your older sister.
My daughters, yes, say to you:
"Our mother's brother, he is Desana.
You, yes, you, yes, our uncle,
How can you stand up
When you seem like a Tukano?
But we are Other People
And that's why you can't stand up to us,"
Say my daughters.
Yahuri Pona, yes, are people who have their head in place,
I say to you.

Dero, a high-ranked Wanano, performed this song in Curideri (Turtle Egg Village), where he was born and remained, where his ancestors lived, and where his sib's ancestral spirit resides. He is a "belonging one." Having conformed in his postmarital residence to principles of patrilocality, he lives among speakers of his own language. Since Dero speaks his own language, an important component of proper identity and placement, he compares himself proudly to the visitor, a Desana who lives at a mission center in Colombia where Tukano is the *lingua franca*. In a conventional citation form, he shifts to his daughter's voice to present a contrast: the mother's brother "seem[s] like a Tukano," because he speaks Tukano, not Desana, as would be proper. The mother's brother is, in this sense, a mixer. High-ranked and in the right place, Dero exemplifies the *makariro*.

His prideful song contains several conventional lines, including the repeated, "I am a person accustomed to taking the calabash." The calabash referred to is the gourd ladle used to serve beer, and the line boasts that he is a seasoned drinker. This may be taken in two ways: first, that Dero has had many such exchanges in his history and is therefore important; and, second, that he is a man who can drink long without showing the effects of alcohol.

Dero speaks for himself and on behalf of his sib when he says that the Yahuri Pona have their "head in place." This refers not only to the anatomical head, but also to rank and authority. Functions of the anatomical head—to lead, organize, speak for the body—are carried out for the Wanano sib by its senior member, and for all Wanano by the "First" sib. Dero's statement that the sib's head is in place expresses several aspects of belonging: proper geographic location; proper physical composition, as compared to images of decomposition in songs of displacement; and proper rank and ability to speak out, "stand," and manifest authority.

Songs of Mixing Females

The women's songs excerpted here exemplify a tradition known cross-culturally as "laments," spontaneous oral poems that convey grief and attempt to move the audience to empathize with the singer. While lament songs are performed by women (and sometimes men) in vastly differing cultures, that which constitutes tragedy is culture-specific. The following songs lend insight into the sources of loss and separation meaningful to the Wanano.

The following song was performed by Tariana wives living in the Wanano village of their husbands. Ria and Cami refer to each other as "sisters" in keeping with the extension of sibling terminology used to address members of the same language group. Having no brothers, they were not married through sister exchange, the preferred mode. Thus, Ria and Cami have not married back, but have married into a group in which they had neither closely related mother's brothers nor father's sisters; for a woman this is the ultimate "passing through" (Wan. *thiniko*). They say, conventionally, that they do not belong; they are "mixing ones."

> Ria: We feel the pain.
> Cami: We are born to remain after our fathers
>   To feel this pain.
> Ria: My younger sister, we who pass through,
>   Only the Tariana women
>   Pass through like this,
>   Seated in places with feelings of pain.

When they speak this way of us, we go,
We Tariana women.

Cami: After my father decomposed beneath the earth,
I pass through, alone, like this.
My forefathers,
Now that you are under the earth I cry after you,
My forefathers.
Tariana women, yes,
As they speak so we wander.

Ria: Another day when I die they will
Throw me out
Because I have no kinsmen.

Cami: My older sister,
Let us drink beer.

The song by Ria and Cami presents stronger images of unbelonging than everyday conversation allows. Cami speaks of her father, "decomposed beneath the earth." Ria responds, "when I die they will throw me out because I have no kinsmen." The image of the progenitor's physical decomposition contrasts with the assertion of intactness—the ancestral "head in place"—found in Dero's song.

Another song expresses the displacement of a woman whose father lives uxorilocally. Unlike "mixing" women who have not married back, Tioda does not even have children to connect her with the Wanano. When it was alleged that Tioda's father, a Cubeo, killed a man in the Querarí area, he left his settlement to reside in the village of his Wanano wife's sib. Living as the only Cubeo family among the Wanano, speaking a language not their own, Tioda and her brother Wado are displaced. Like other women who do not belong, Tioda chooses a bird to symbolize her wandering. She likens herself to the *kairoro*, a bird said to "sing in all the languages of the world."

She sings the following song in Wanano to a Wanano cross-cousin during a visit to the settlement of her mother's brothers:

The way I am
No one can tolerate
Because I am like a heartache.
I say this to you as I tease you,
My cousin,
No one can tolerate the way I am.
I say this to you because I am sad . . .
I am as the *kairoro* bird.

I am as one who wanders . . .
As though I were with longing and sadness.
So I seem.
I alone say this to you, my cousin,
Because I am a Cubeo woman who mixes in the middle of you.

Song of a Mixing Male

Tioda's brother illustrates that a man may also be designated a "mixing one." In the song excerpted here, Wado sings in Wanano to a Wanano female cross-cousin of the hosting Wiroa sib in the village of Soma:

All night long
I sing this way
For the Wiroa women
Who don't like me because I am Cubeo . . .
In the river, long,
The Cubeo passes here and goes there.
The Wiroa women don't like
That I am Cubeo, Cubeo, Cubeo, I am,
Passing through their midst.
When the day dawns
On Crocodile Waterfall
In a still pool
I will be
As a *bu?sanaikúro* [a minnow]
I will be singing here and there,
I say this to you my cousin . . .
Here at Crocodile Falls, above the waterfall,
I sing this way . . .
When the white foam appears in the waterfall—
There I pass by,
Like the foam in the river,
Moving here, moving there. . . .
Thus am I
Singing in your midst.
. . . We are Cubeo,
And you Wanano
Do not like the Cubeo.
"[Wiroa women] are not going to tolerate you,
My brother," says my sister,
My only sister

Who lives alone on the island—
People think about her with deep sorrow,
As though she were a *minia kairoro.*
That sings alone on the island . . .
I arrived here, I learned Wanano, and
I am the grandson of Diani.
For this reason I learned to speak Wanano
But I am not speaking properly.

While Dero, a "belonging one," sang of having his head in place, Wado "passes through" like the small *bu?sanaiküro* fish. His displacement is experienced in terms of language as well. Although a Cubeo, Wado started to speak Wanano, detaching himself from his language of identity. As the grandson of Diani, he recognized a matrilineal link to a Wanano sib ancestor, yet he is "not speaking properly" as he would if he belonged. His ancestors do not fall properly before him.

Wado expresses his displacement through the symbols of still water (discontinuity) and rapid running water (frantic wandering). These images assume additional meaning in light of the central Uaupés origin account in which each language group and each sib emerges from a segment of a primordial anaconda at the site of its linguistically associated descent group. If ever Wado was placed properly along the river, he is not so placed now. Like his sister, he belongs nowhere.

Reflecting the Wanano view of his sister's displacement, Wado sings that she is a wanderer too. The people say she lives "alone on the island" and "sings alone." With no place or people, she is stigmatized and isolated. People regard her as a bird that sings in all of the languages of the world. Since language indicates group affiliation and thus social placement, this image suggests an ultimate form of mixing.

Song to a Belonging Female

In the following song, two members of the Tukano language group sing to one another in the Wanano village in which they both live. (They refer to one another as "sister" and "brother" in keeping with the extension of sibling terms to all members of the language group.) Both have married into the village in which they live. For the female, this conventional arrangement carries proper placement since Vitu has married into her mother's sib. For the male, however, it is improper. Because of a dispute Tono's father had left his own sib's settlement years before and had come to live with his wife's family. As an adult, Tono married one of his mother's brother's daughters and continued to live with her family. Tono sings to Vitu:

Why do you fear beer and drink?
Take this.
Take this serving gourd.
You are here by proper heritage from your grandfather.
You are rightfully from here; you have rights.
Sing to me, woman of here.
Sing this to me.
Sing to me, you who are rightfully from here.

Living uxorilocally, Tono describes himself as "ugly" and a "passerby." Vitu, in contrast, is a "belonging one." Their mothers are both from the village in which they have married and reside; therefore, both marriages are proper. But Tono tells Vitu that she is "rightfully from here" and "truly belonging"—"here by heritage," while he has a father from elsewhere and therefore "moves about."

From Belonging to Nonbelonging: Changing Status

Later, in chapter 10, we will closely examine the case of a woman who is displaced and sings about her predicament. Her song demonstrates well the indivisibility of time and space in the Wanano concept of placement. As the last remaining member of the highest-ranking Wanano sib, the Biari Pona, Nicho has lost all temporal connection with her place. She sings the following song after fleeing the settlement her sib had once dominated, to seek the advice of a shaman. She is, in this way, both a literal and a figurative wanderer.

. . . Alone am I,
I have no brothers.
Like a bird that goes
Here and there,
Dragging her offspring with her,
Sons, who are Other people
My oldest son says . . .
"Like a horsefly
With its eye plucked out,
You fly here and there
Alone,
Because you are alone."

Nicho compares herself to a horsefly with its eyes plucked, flying blindly here and there. This implies movement not only in space, but also in time. Nicho's song describes figuratively her futile attempt to connect with her ancestry. A sense of belonging had emanated from temporal links connecting Nicho to her father and his fathers. Now that the lineage is disrupted, Nicho does not belong, and as a wanderer she carries the fate of her progeny with her.

Sib Litanies

We now turn to a different type of performance mode, the sib litany. Like the secular songs, sib litanies are performed during visits between two sibs. But whereas the secular songs are sung by nonspecialists and may take place anywhere in the dance house, litanies are sacred and represent the esoteric knowledge of the sib seniors. They are chanted only by the senior member of the hosting sib, who sits alone on a sacred stool at a designated place on the men's side of the house. And whereas secular songs are improvised, the text of the sib litany is a (theoretically) unalterable ceremonial statement.

In these sacred chants a sib commemorates its ancestors and reinforces group solidarity and continuity. Performance is a sacred act whose goal is the transcendence of the profane present: the lives of the ancestors and the present sib members become one in a metaphysical and social sense.

The litany's contents reflect this goal. Diachronic exchange is its foremost theme. Exchange among the Wanano is the mode through which interaction occurs between properly placed social entities, whether they be individuals or groups. Synchronic exchange occurs in various spheres of social life, including the exchange of marriage partners, languages, or material goods. Diachronic exchange involves the receipt of an ancestor's name, which breathes life into an individual; through the name, the ancestor endows the recipient with a right to social existence, as well as a particular placement and a concomitant set of social, economic, and ritual privileges. The recipient, in exchange, owes the ancestor, and the social group, the responsibility of living up to the name. To a Wanano, the bearer of an ancestral name is the "exchange" for that ancestor, his present incarnation. In this way, ancestor and descendant exchange life-giving acts. This exchange principle cycles ranked names down through the generations, abolishing time and perpetuating rank order.

The texts of sib litanies illustrate how the categories of belonging/mixing, sitting/being, and exchange are related. To belong, a

Wanano must first exhibit the quality of *duhisina*, "sitting-being." One can sit in a place only through the proper exchange, for the soul (*yeheripona*, "heart" or "soul") is regenerated by the ancestor's "return."[2] One sib litany begins:

Sit yet in this place . . .
This Dianumia [sib ancestor] did so.
This Dianumia also sat in this place to which his soul returned.

Another sacred chant emphasizes the same theme and refers to sib ancestors:

Each one was in his place, sitting and waiting for the talk . . .
My soul returned with a beautiful cigar-holder,
Indeed my heart has returned.

Sitting is associated with permanence or continuity in space. The Wanano believe that the spirit must return to the place where it is born. The ancestral place must correspond to the descendant sib members' place, for only through order and continuity of lineage may the spirit return. Objects of mediation, such as a sacred cigar in an ancestral cigar-holder, facilitate exchange. Proper performance of the litany, with tobacco smoke as a visible sign of the sacred breath, results in sitting-being, for the "heart" or "soul" has returned.

Once a sib is properly placed, then, the living world and ancestral realm are bridged. The heart, breath, and soul return. These are the central elements of "sitting-being"—the requisites of belonging. Only this posture can bring tranquility and social order.

Conclusion

Societies produce models of their own situations, then live and define roles according to these models. As Sherry Ortner states, "A culture is the system of such publicly and collectively subscribed-to-models operating for a given group at a given period of time—the system of terms, forms, categories, images, and the like which function to interpret a people's own situation to themselves" (1975: 133).

Placement—a spatial dimension of personhood—is a key concept in the cultural system by which the Wanano interpret themselves. The concept is realized in metaphor, imagery, and myth. The lyrical correlatives to the concept of placement cited here demonstrate the integrity and indivisibility of person, place, and time in Wanano thought.

PART III: ECOLOGY AND ECONOMY

Chapter 7. The Succulence of Place: Control and Distribution of Fish Resources

THE EARLY CHAPTERS OF THIS STUDY describe the conceptual models underlying Wanano social organization, with particular attention to the organizing principle of rank. Subsequent chapters present two incidents that occurred during fieldwork, which exemplify the operation of rank on the ground, as well as the tensions and negotiations associated with it. These chapters show that, conceptually, rank is associated with the image of the head and with succulence and that rank becomes manifest through demonstrated succulence, that is, through public displays of generosity.

This dynamic raises questions taken up in this chapter: how do those of high rank maintain privileged access to more abundant resources and thus remain succulent? How is the expectation of generosity perpetuated? To approach these issues, we must turn our attention to the Uaupés environment and to the Wanano means of exploiting it to produce subsistence-level and surplus food supplies.

According to a comparative survey carried out by Robert Carneiro (1970), the Tukano rely more heavily on fishing than any other group of Amazonian Indians (based upon data derived from the Cubeo Tukano, Goldman 1963). This reliance on fish is exceptional for a group located on a tributary stream, where fish are expected to be less abundant and the size of individual fish smaller (Meggers 1971). Furthermore, the Tukano demonstrate a greater density of settlement than do Amerindian populations elsewhere in Amazonia, a density perhaps permitted by their heavy reliance on fish.

Wanano men are fishermen; the women are horticulturalists. Manioc, the carbohydrate staple, provides the bulk of caloric intake. Wild fruits and insects make a contribution to the diet, but fish is the mainstay, accounting for more than 90 percent of protein.

Because land is abundant, the amount of available labor rather than location determines the quantity of manioc harvested and processed by a sib. Although the land is not particularly fertile, locations do not differ significantly from one another in this respect. The abundance of wild fruit, but most importantly of fishing yields, therefore, provides the best means for assessing the relative productivity of different localities and for determining how these factors relate to rank.

The first part of this chapter describes fluctuations in environmental factors that result in different productivity levels, or relative "abundance," in various locales. More specifically, it relates Uaupés fishing yields to these fluctuations. Finally, it evaluates the Wanano association of rank with abundance in terms of these factors. The next section continues the discussion of hierarchy and productivity by elaborating on fishing practices and comparing various means of organizing, controlling, and distributing production.

Rainfall and Water Level

The location of the Uaupés at the northwest extreme of the basin places it within Amazonia's area of maximum rainfall. For example, for the years 1965–1974, the average yearly rainfall in the central Uaupés was 3,743 mm (Ministério das Minas e Energia 1976). This level of annual precipitation is high, even relative to other locations in the Amazon basin.

A second striking feature of the Uaupés basin is its flooding regime. The Uaupés system floods and drains twice annually (see fig. 6) as opposed to the single annual flood that typifies the rest of the basin. Because of its location near the equator, the Uaupés is subject to two rainy seasons—a northern and a southern. As the contribution of one tributary system slackens, the other intensifies. Flood peaks generally occur in the months of October and April, alternating with low-water periods, although each year produces some variation in this pattern.

The River

The Uaupés River flows over the geologically ancient Guiana shield. The impoverished granitic and gneissic parent material generates soils (called spodosols and psamments) that are characteristically acidic and weathered (table 8). They are deficient in important inorganic ions such as nitrogen and phosphorus, but rich in organic humic compounds, which impart a dark brown color to the associated groundwater and outflowing streams.

Since blackwater rivers do not contain the levels of nutrients necessary for *in situ* production of large amounts of primary phytoplankton, these rivers are of limited primary productivity (table 9).

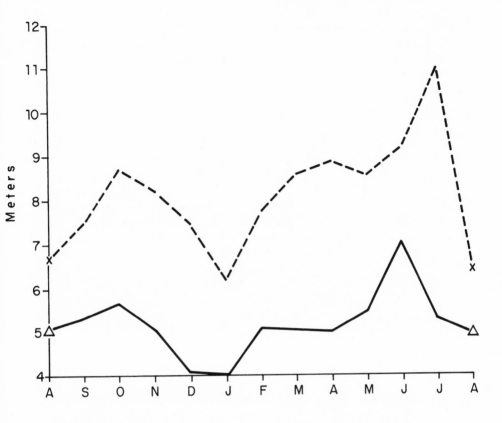

Figure 6. Maximum and minimum water levels from August 1980 to August 1981, Iauaretê Cachoeira, Uaupés River.

Table 8. *Mean Values for Nutrient Contents of Soils Sampled at 25 Locations in the Uaupés River Basin*

Phosphorus (p.p.m.)	Potassium (mE/100g)	Calcium & Magnesium (mE/100g)	Aluminum (mE/100g)	pH
6.56 (low)	41.48 (low)	0.57 (low)	1.5 (high)	4.6 (acidic)

Samples collected by the author from October 1 to November 30, 1979; longitude 1°10′N; latitude 69°50′ to 69°80′W.

Table 9. *Limnochemical Characteristics of the*
Uaupés River, Brazil

ph	Ca mg/l	Mg mg/l	Na mg/l	K mg/l	Fe (sol.) mg/l	Fe (comp.) mg/l
4.1	0.00	0.54	0.25	0.27	0.09	0.91

Note: These data, collected by the author at Iauareté Cachoeira, 1979–1980, are reported in Santos et al. 1984 and Chernela 1989a.

They have been referred to as "rivers of hunger." In blackwater rivers such as the Uaupés, with depauperate primary production, the major sources of biomass in the system are external. The single most important contributor of nutrients is the surrounding forest.[1]

With the *in situ* nutrient supply low, fish are dependent upon plant and animal parts that fall into the water from the adjacent forest or are engulfed by the waters during the rising floods (Knoppel 1970; Goulding 1980). Input from the terrestrial fringes into the river—such as insects, larvae, arachnids, worms, crustaceans—and numerous types of plant matter—including fruits, seeds, wood, leaves, stems, flowers, pollen, and microflora—enter the aquatic system as floating debris, mud, and detritus.

The dynamics of this system are especially dramatic during the two highwater seasons. With flooding, the rivers swell and overflow their banks, merging the aquatic with the terrestrial realms. It is in these two seasons that fish gorge themselves—spreading through the flooded forest and feeding on the abundance of forest foods only then available.

These features are important to blackwater Uaupés fishermen, such as the Wanano. As fishermen dependent upon these river systems, the Wanano are aware of the relationship between their environment and the life cycles of fish, particularly the role played by the adjacent forest in providing nutrient sources that maintain vital fisheries (Chernela 1989a). Wanano proscriptions prohibit deforestation of the river margin because it is viewed as part of the aquatic system, reserved as feeding grounds belonging to the fish.

Biotopes

The Wanano have long recognized a wide variety of biotopes in the Uaupés region. With regard to fishing, the three most important biotopes are: *igapós*, cataracts, and *terra firme*.

Table 9.
(*continued*)

Fe (total) mg/l	Mn mg/l	P mg/l	N (org) mg/l	Cl mg/l	Si mg/l	Al mg/l
1.00	0.00	0.02	0.79	0.71	2.68	1.54

Igapós *and* Terra Firme

The river margins can be divided into uplands (*terra firme*), which are never submerged, and *igapós*, floodplains that are lower in elevation and subject to seasonal immersion.[2] As Nigel Smith (1981) shows, the biological productivity of water bordered by *terra firme* is minimal in comparison to that of floodplain areas.

The dramatic and sudden input of available food due to flooding in the *igapó* is illustrated by calculations of the leaf fall per hectare in one year. If the leaf fall from each tree is 20 lbs. annually, one hectare with 600 trees would produce six tons of leaf fall in the course of one year. Data I derived on fish capture in the Uaupés river basin further illustrate the relative productivity of the flooded forest. These findings show that the average weight per fish obtained in flooded forests was 363.5 grams as compared to 91.5 grams per fish captured in nonflood seasons in uplands.

Cataracts

The Uaupés River runs through gently undulating lowland terrain. The bed is generally composed of sand or clay. Where the river channel encounters erosion-resistant granite outcroppings, cataracts occur. There are some thirty major cataracts (also called cascades) and sixty smaller rapids on the main course of the river. These cataracts act as a series of locks along the river course, resulting in stretches of level water interspersed with rapid-flowing water.

The distinctive cataract habitat supports a specialized fauna adapted to rigorous conditions of rapid water flow, high turbulence, and oxygen saturation. The rocks offer both shelter and food for the fish. They provide a substrate on which algae and aquatic higher plants grow. The plant communities in turn house large quantities of insect larvae on which fishes feed. These factors and the shelter for fishes result in relatively high biomass.

Cataract-dwelling fishes[3] may be described as sedentary, as compared to those inhabiting the middle of the water column, which are more typically in motion (Hynes 1970). Fishes tend to live close to the substratum where the current is greatly reduced or in the crevices between rocks. Open-water fishes often travel in shoals for protection, whereas cataract-dwelling species utilize the crevices of rocks for shelter. A rocky area, with its complex ecosystem, and specifically with its protective crevices, permits more fishes to occupy a given volume than do open waters.

The highest cataracts with steepest gradients are permanent, whereas lower cataracts, which typically have less pronounced gradients, are seasonal, disappearing during high-water periods. The cataract's height is the determinate feature in its function as a barrier to certain fishes. The degree of interchange across cataracts is determined by the height of the outcropping and the degree to which it extends across the river channel. Permanent cataracts act as boundaries in the faunal distributions of certain species. Each succeeding cataract blocks numerous large fishes, which, lacking the ability to forge the powerful rapids, never reach the Uaupés basin.

The cataract blocks water passage in such a way that fishes passing through it are funneled through a limited number of discrete channels. This feature affects Wanano fishing practices, since channels appear and disappear predictably with the seasonal rise and fall in water levels. Trap locations are subject to these variables, as we will see.

We may summarize this discussion of fish habitats as follows:

1. The blackwater river is a fairly sterile environment whose food resources derive from outside the river system;

2. Two habitats are more productive for fishing than others: flooded forests, which provide fish with vast quantities of otherwise unavailable foods; and cataracts, whose greater protective surfaces and crevices permit more fishes to occupy a given space than open waters and whose aquatic plant and associated faunal communities provide greater food sources;

3. The salient feature of this environment is the appearance and disappearance of certain aquatic habitats with river level fluctuation.

These cyclical changes are predictable within limits. Wanano methods of fish capture take into account the fishes' feeding, reproductive, and migratory cycles that result from the pronounced seasonal fluctuations in the ecology of the river system.

Resource Access at Different Locations

Comparative Fishing Yields

We now turn to the Wanano use of fishery resources in relation to various types of habitat.[4]

Data based on fishing observations carried out over one year demonstrate the dramatic variation in actual yield per habitat type. Figures 7 and 8 illustrate the dramatically high percentage of fish captured in areas of seasonally flooded forests as opposed to other habitats. Cataracts provide the next highest biomass of captured fish. Together, cataract and seasonally flooded forests (*igapó*) account for more than 80 percent of fish captured. Waters adjacent to *terra firme* yielded the fewest fishes in terms of both numbers and total biomass.

Sib Rank and Control of Fishing Sites

The Wanano association of rank with abundance would suggest that higher-ranked sibs would inhabit locations with more abundant food supplies—particularly fish, the primary protein source and the most highly valued food. On examination, this turns out to be the case.

As noted, the data show that the most productive habitats are, first, flooded forests, and, second, cataracts. Together, these sites account for 80 percent of all fish captured.

Sibs' proprietary rights to specific locations are fixed on the basis of ancestral emergence from the primordial anaconda. They restrict fishing within their boundaries to sib members and certain visitors. Great variation is found in the access of sibs to different habitats.

Social Ideology and Settlement

According to Wanano ideology, sibs are arranged along the river as the first ancestors, *pamori mahsa,* emerged from the body of the ancestral anaconda. The senior groups are thought to have emerged from the head of the anaconda and the junior groups from the tail. Accordingly, the most chiefly sibs should be located downriver; the less chiefly, in descending order, should be situated upriver.

In fact, among the Wanano the more chiefly groups are located downriver; no senior groups are found upriver. Occupation of these sites is legitimized by myths of several kinds, including that of the anaconda. In addition, each chiefly sib has its own origin myth, in

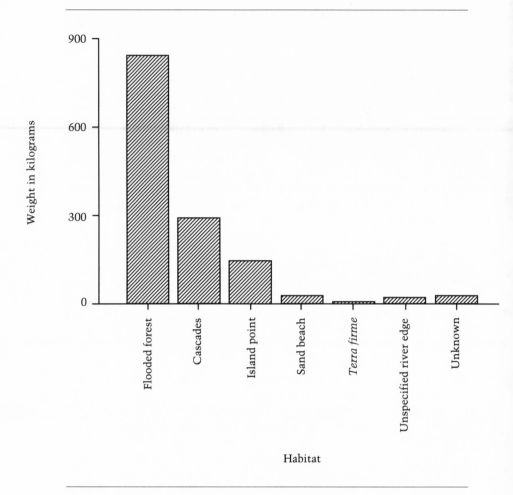

Figure 7. Total weight of fish caught, by habitat (based on 1,910 observed fishing man-hours for 25 fishermen over one year).

which its first ancestor appears at the sib's site, leaving signs of his occupation in markings in the site's landscape, most typically in stone. Furthermore, chiefly sibs have litanies which repeat the sib order, and which they recite to visiting younger brother groups. These sib litanies stress "sitting" in the ancestral "sitting place," for only in this way can the ancestral soul return.

However, the alignment of groups departs from the strict downriver/senior, upriver/junior pattern in the following ways. First, sibs designated as "servants" live among chiefly sibs downriver. Some

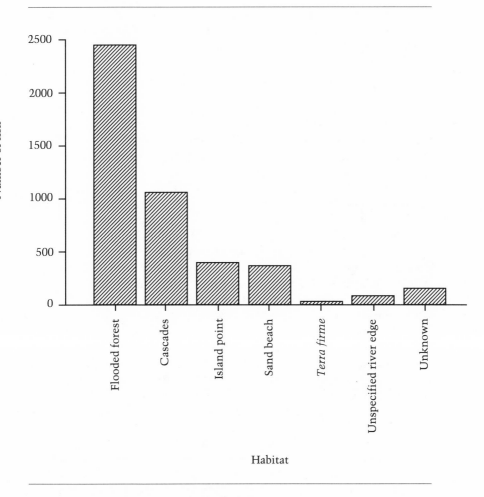

Figure 8. Number of fish caught, by habitat.

live in chiefly settlements, and others live in nearby associated settlements. However, each servant sib is thought to be paired with a
chiefly sib, having come to the settlement at an earlier time at the
senior group's invitation. These servants, or Wiroa, are thought to
have originated not with the anaconda canoe, but later, at the hands
of an ancestral Wanano shaman. They are the grandfather groups,
living among the grandchildren groups.

Second, there are exceptions to the correspondence of sib order
with order on the river. For example, the currently highest-ranked

group occupies the most upriver location of the chiefly groups. This exception is best explained by the differences in available resources at various sites.

Sib Location and Environmental Biotypes

Since the productive *igapó* (seasonally flooded forests) and cataract habitats may be exploited in alternate seasons, the most advantageous location would afford access to both. The second most desirable site would have access to one habitat or the other. The next best site would offer river frontage.

The least preferable site would be one without either cataracts or seasonally flooded forests, located at a margin of *terra firme*. The least advantageous location would allow no legitimate control of river resources.

On the main channel of the Uaupés and on its largest tributary, the Papurí, the portion of forest subject to inundation is small relative to the nonflooded uplands (see fig. 9). On the Tiquiê the situation is reversed. From its confluence with the Papurí to the Colombian frontier, the Uaupés River stretches 175 km. Only 12 percent (22 km) of its river margin is *igapó*, subject to flooding in high waters. The remaining 88 percent drains nonflooded high ground. The Papurí River is 154 km in length from its mouth to the Colombian border. Only 11 percent (17 km) of it is subject to flooding. In contrast, 91 percent of the 450 km through which the Tiquiê River runs, from its mouth to its entrance into Colombia, drains seasonally flooded forests.

The Wanano area with which I am familiar encompasses only one flooded forest. The territory controlled by the highest-ranked sib includes that flooded forest and two cataracts. The flooded forest at Tucunare Igarapê near Yapima, estimated on the basis of satellite photographs to cover 190 km² (site A, fig. 9), formerly belonged to the Biari Pona, first-ranked sib at Bucacopa. Since the demise of the Biari Pona over the last two generations, it has been occupied by the next highest ranked sib.

On the Papurí, the only flooded forest is located at Sta. Luzia at the mouth of Turí Igarapé. The highest-ranked sib of the Tukano language group inhabits this site, controlling both that flooded forest and a very large waterfall (site B, fig. 9).

On the Tiquiê, where the river's lower reaches meander through flooded forests, the highest-ranked group—a Tukano sib—is located at Pari Cachoeira, the site of the most downstream cascade, and has within its fishing territories both flooded forests and cascades

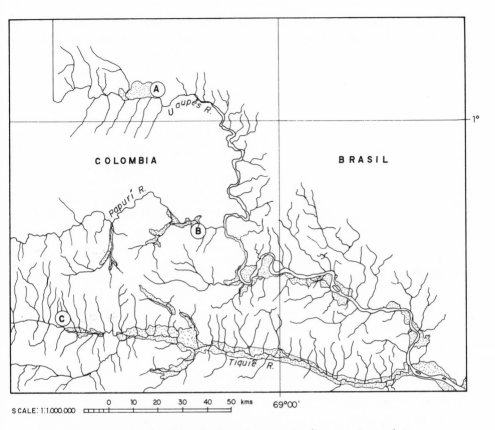

Figure 9. Locations of high-ranked settlements in three sections of river (based on Landsat images, Ministério das Minas e Energia 1976).

(site C, fig. 9). On each one of these river segments, the highest-ranked sibs control both cascades and flooded forests.

Furthermore, each of the numerous cascades that punctuate the Wanano stretch of the Uaupés belongs to one of the first-ranked sibs—the Wamisima—by virtue of their ancestors' emergence at that site from the ancestral canoe. Each Wamisima settlement is located at one of these cascades.

Upriver from these sites are the settlements of the Tibahana, the second brothers or uncles. These sites are located on *terra firme* stretches of river, with neither flooded forests nor cascades. Only one, Taracua, is located near minor rapids that appear in the low-water season.

The Wiroa, described by the Wamisima as "servants," are considered to have no legitimate control over river frontage. Downriver, they live among the Wamisima (first brothers) and are thought to be paired with the Wamisima sibs in a grandchild/grandparent relation. In some settlements, such as Yapima, they occupy a separate affiliated village and maintain utilization rights over one of the Yapima cascades.

Seniority and Sib River Placement

Seniority is thus commensurate with social "succulence" and related to geographic "placement." For seniors to behave "seniorly" they must occupy highly productive sites. The fundamental expression of seniority as succulence is manifested and reiterated in the succulence of nature: the one identifies the other (Chernela 1985a, b).

Harnessing the Gift: Wanano Fishing Methods and Resource Control

Likewise, within a local settlement, certain fishing sites are the property of the sib and under control of the chiefly line. As we will see, these allow them to carry on their chiefly functions. Productivity and site are related, but only in terms of specific technologies.

Chapter 9 describes the dilemma of a chief who lacks access to the chiefly fishweir. This section reports a number of fishing methods, demonstrating that: (1) different sites are productive at various times and under varying conditions; (2) some methods are more efficient in terms of input-output ratios; and (3) certain sites are effectively controlled. The information on fishing was gathered over one year.[5]

The Wanano utilize a wide variety of fishing techniques that I have organized into ten categories. These may be generally divided into search-and-capture methods and fixed facility methods.

Search-and-Capture Methods

Seven techniques—utilizing an array of fishing gear and suited to a variety of conditions—require fishermen first to locate and then to capture their prey.

Bow-and-Arrow Fishing (buedu). Bow-and-arrow fishing is practiced in daylight in waters less than a meter in depth. The shaft and point of the arrow are carved from wood, with one or two barbs at the sharpened point. The method is used in the low-water season as well as in the shallow areas of flooded forests during high-water periods. This method prevails only in March and April (a high-water period) in the flooded forests and in July–September (a low-water period) in shallow streams.

Several interesting baiting techniques are associated with bow-and-arrow fishing in the flooded forest. For example, a fisherman may grate a fragrant fruit, such as *waso* (*Couma guianensis*, fam. Apocynaceae, or *sorva* in *língua geral*) or manioc paste, wrap it loosely in a leaf, and tie the leaf with a vine. He dips the ball into the water several times, allowing the juices to seep out. He then waits and prepares to shoot any fish attracted by the bait.

Other techniques make use of naturally occurring attractants. A fisherman may place his canoe in the flooded forest under a tree bearing ripe fruit, waiting with bow and arrow to shoot fishes that feed on falling or floating fruit. The favored fruits of fishes are thought to be the species *wa?i pati* (Euphorbiaceae, tentatively *Mabia caudata*), *wa?i pa* (*Byrsonima*, fam. Malpighiceae), and *dia simi* (*Macrolobium multijugium*, fam. Leguminosae). A fisherman may also wait near a well-situated termite nest in a log or stump, catching various types of *aracú* (*Leporinus* sp.), which feed on termites.

Spear Fishing (*nyosansi?ne*). This method is carried out at night using flashlight and wooden spears with multiple-pronged heads. No bait is needed. *Tucunaré* (*Cichla ocellaris*), *traíra* (*Hoplias malabaricus*), *cará* (*Geophagus surinamensis*), and *aracú* (*Leporinus* sp.) are captured in this way. Like bow-and-arrow fishing, spearing must be done in shallow water—for example, in shallowly flooded forests. In the absence of flooded forests, both methods may be limited to the dry season, when shallow waters are more common.

Net Fishing (*yakaho?na*). A net woven from palm fiber (*tucum*), 1 or 2 m in diameter, is required for this method. Its rim is rigid yet flexible, allowing the fisherman to manipulate its shape so that it may serve as a strainer, stop net, or dip net. Its use is highly specific to habitat, time of day, and season. From July to September the nets are set just before dawn between rocks in rapids to capture the fishes as they attempt to leave the protection of the crevices between the rocks. They are also used in March and April to lift fishes out of flooded forests.

Drag-Line Fishing. This appears to be an introduced technique: a heavy-duty fishing line with a large hook and a variety of bait is attached to a wooden float. The Wanano rarely use this technique, probably because of the difficulty of obtaining the necessary gear.[6]

It is used only in July and August when fishermen attempt to capture the large catfish *piraíba* (*Brachyplatystoma filamentosum*). The largest catfish I saw during my visit, 1.75 m long, was one of several caught by the drag-line method.

Hand Fishing. Hand and machete are occasionally used to capture fishes but they are exceptional or occasional rather than major methods of capture. A few fishes were captured by hand and machete in March in flooded forests.

The Wanano utilize a wide repertoire of hook techniques, which I have divided into two groupings: hook-and-line and snare techniques.

Hook-and-Line Fishing. Fishing with hand line, set line, trot line, or rod-and-line is included in this category. The hook may be whittled from a branch, or a fisherman may use a manufactured hook or an improvised steel hook formed from a nail or safety pin. The line is forest vine or nylon.

Snare Fishing. Snare techniques are numerous and widely used. In general, a flexible sapling at the river edge is pulled down by a string attached to a triggered line with a baited hook. The fish need only nibble on the bait to trigger the release mechanism, pulling the sapling—and the fish—out of the water. Frequently, snare traps are arranged in a series along a stream bank, a method known as *yoga poa*.

Snare and hook methods make use of various types of bait, most commonly fruit from the families Apocynaceae, Euphorbiaceae, and Leguminosae. Manioc paste, spiders, ants, worms, and crickets are also used. In contrast to the seasonal specificity of the other methods, hook and snare methods are viable year-round. They are used during months when other techniques are not feasible or by fishermen who do not have access to all methods.

Fixed Fishing Facilities

Fixed facility methods differ from search-and-capture techniques: once the trap is installed, the fisherman need only harvest the fish; no search period is involved. Three types of weirs or fish installations are used.

Basket Trap (*bühküyaka*). This cylindrical trap is a basket, approximately 0.5 m in diameter at the mouth and up to 2 m long, which is set in a fence. The fence is a barrier of bamboo or saplings placed across the narrow openings between the large rocks in rapids or between areas of high ground in flooded forests. They may be set

Figure 10a. Basket trap.

Figure 10b. Basket trap fence at cataract showing one opening for trap (upper level), no longer seasonable, and lower openings with traps in place.

Figure 10c. Basket traps set in fence.

in cataracts during rising water or in flooded forests during receding waters. In rising-water seasons, the basket traps' openings face downstream to capture fishes swimming upstream against the current. In this way, they are extremely important during fish migrations. The traps capture fishes as they are channeled through the few waterways not blocked by rocky outcrops.

When the water is receding, basket traps are placed, openings facing upstream, in strategic locations in flooded forests where passages narrow. They intercept fishes as they return with the downstream current to the main river. Fishes enter the forest with the rising water and disperse to spawn or feed on the abundant new foods available. As the waters recede, the dispersed fishes and their predators are increasingly concentrated into fast-flowing currents that run through deeper channels between emerging islands of *terra firme*. During this period, water flow from the river onto the land is reversed as several temporary canals emerge, draining water back into the river. The fishermen install basket traps in these canals.

Wing Trap (waʔiro). The *waʔiro* is a large stationary trap set on a rocky substratum at the margin of the river or at an island point. The installations, which reach 3 m high and 40 m long, consist of felled logs arranged into a double-V-shaped capture chamber. A wing is extended from the apex at the river edge out into the river channel to draw fishes into the chamber. The trap is designed to capture fishes swimming upriver along the margin or feeding at the margin.

Platform Trap (kaya). A *kaya* is a large platform trap built over a waterfall. In this position, it exploits the turbulent upward thrust of standing waves at the waterfall. The *kaya* catches fishes swimming downriver or upriver that are forced upward by rapid-running water as the water level rises or falls. Some but not all platform traps can be used even at the flood peak.

Poison

This method does not fall easily into either the fixed facility or search-and-capture category. When the waters are lowest, fishermen close off drying streams with leafy branches and apply fish poisons in the enclosed areas. The poisons—plant toxins derived from stems, roots, leaves, or fruits—are crushed, mixed with clay, and poured into drying streams. Trapped fish are debilitated and easily captured. Unlike many other fishing techniques, poisoning is a community activity. Each member of the community retains the catch he or she has gathered with a hand-dip net.

Figure 11a. Wing trap.

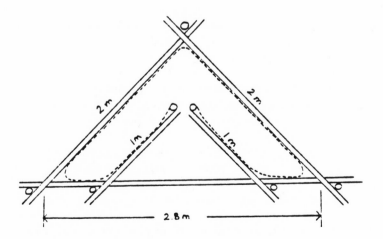

Figure 11b. Aerial view of interior structure.

Figure 12. Platform trap.

Comparative Yields of Fishing Methods per Man-Hour

Overall Findings

Analysis of my data indicates an average yield per man-hour of 570 grams when all methods are combined. This figure was derived by dividing total fish biomass captured by total number of man-hours spent in fishing expeditions, fixed trap construction, and harvesting and maintenance of fixed facilities. However, the productivities of the various techniques vary greatly. Yields produced by a single technique vary between seasons. For example, the productivity of hook-and-line fishing ranged from 220 grams per man-hour in July to 780 grams per man-hour in September.

Figure 13 shows the comparative yields per man-hour for each fishing method. The two hook methods (snare and hook-and-line) produced the lowest average yields per man-hour—less than 500 grams. The average yield per hour with the rarely used hand net was 1,600 grams—more than three times that amount.

In general, fixed facility methods produced consistently higher average yields per man-hour than search-and-capture methods; 1.6 kg for the wing trap; 1.7 kg for the basket trap; and 2.1 kg for the platform trap.

Labor Input in Construction of Fixed Facilities

Fixed facility fishing differs from search-and-capture methods in a number of ways. The installations are large and must be stable. Construction is labor-intensive and requires the cooperation of at least two fishermen. I observed and recorded labor inputs for each type of fixed facility. In the construction of a wing trap whose triangular chamber was 2 m on each side, three men working together invested a total of 55 man-hours. A sum total of 320 man-hours was needed to build a platform trap 10 m in length; this figure represents the combined labor of 11 men over a four-day period. Their labor was observed hourly, and a record was kept of numbers of workers. A basket trap 2 by 0.5 m was constructed in 14 hours by one man. Several of these traps are placed in barricade fences. The figure for labor does not include construction of the wall of saplings woven with vine, which serves as a barricade funneling fish into the trap. The labor required for this task depends on the size of the wall; approximately 1.25 man-hours are required for each meter in length. The wall may run from 1 or 2 m to virtually any size. Maintenance of these walls, although fairly frequent, is not time-consuming.

The total labor invested within a short period is apparently high; but when divided by the number of participants, labor input per worker is relatively low. For example, labor investment in the building of the platform trap was great; it amounted to 320 hours. However, when these hours are divided by the 11 participating builders who will share in the harvest, the investment is a reasonable 29 hours per person. This investment may be compared to the duration of one man's hook-and-line fishing trip, which lasted 79 hours.

Once the initial labor investment is made, the fixed facility requires minimal effort. It is harvested easily and ordinarily requires little maintenance over one season. Even when the original labor inputs are considered, yields per unit time of fixed facility fishing are dramatically high.

Social Control of Fishing Facilities

Individual skill is an important factor in certain methods, particularly in hook-and-line fishing. In fixed facility fishing, on the other hand, trap placement, not individual skill, is the significant variable in total yield. Social factors granting the use of these facilities

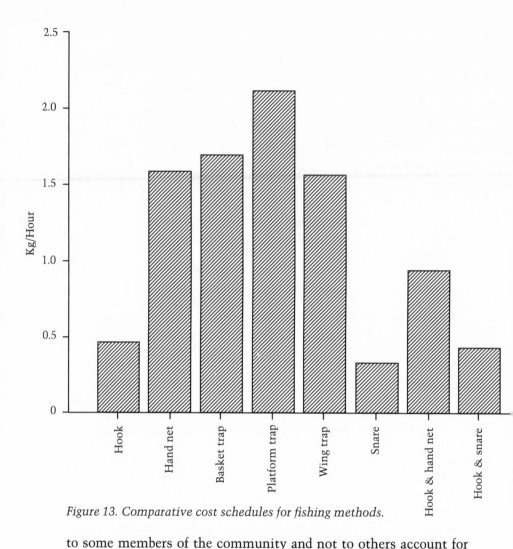

Figure 13. Comparative cost schedules for fishing methods.

to some members of the community and not to others account for the discrepancies in individual yields. In December 1978, for instance, individual productivity ranged from .0017 kg to 7.01 kg per man-hour. The wide range reflects the fact that only the sib's highest-ranking members have access to the most productive fishing techniques, the fixed facilities. Individual productivity with fixed facility methods proved to be independent of age and skill, as several examples will illustrate. Pilo, a 12-year-old boy from a high-ranking family, harvested a catch from his family's wing trap in April 1979. His productivity, 1.299 kg per hour, exceeded that of all other fishermen observed in that month. In December 1978, Makisi and Kinto were the only fishermen in the village of Mo with basket trap sites. Despite the fact that these two men are very old, and Makisi has only one leg, they were the most productive fishermen observed in that month. Although Makisi had eleven children and was the sole supporting fisherman for his household, he invited me to live with them, which I did. An additional mouth to feed was no burden. In the month during which I recorded their activities, Kinto averaged 7.0 kg per hour, and Makisi, 4.70 kg per hour. Kinto's productivity was eleven times that of the next most productive fisherman, while Makisi produced more than eight times as many kilos per hour as that fisherman.

Access to Productive Sites

We have seen that fixed facilities generally produce a greater yield (in biomass) per man-hour than other methods and that their yields depend not on the fisherman's skill or strength, but on trap placement. As a consequence of variations in water level, the productive period of any trap is always temporary, though some are productive for longer periods than others. Those closest to the river channel's deepest sections have the first opportunity to capture fish during rising water, but they are also the first to become submerged. Those in shallower waters, often closest to the river margin or located at high passages between rocks, are the last to become submerged but the first to lose effectiveness as water levels drop.

Because different traps have varied effectiveness as the river gradually and cyclically rises and falls, it is advantageous to install several traps that are functional in consecutive seasons. I know of one village chief who set enough traps at points in the river of varying heights that he was able to harvest fish from one trap or another year-round.

In general, fixed facilities furthest downstream are the most desirable. Migrating fishes and their pursuing predators arrive at the downstream gates before reaching those upstream. Where consecutive weirs are set across the full breadth of the river, enough traps and closures may be created by the downstream weirs to impede the upstream progress of a significant percentage of fish. The downstream weirs thus have a decided advantage, in much the same way that irrigated farms closest to a water source have an advantage over sites further away.

Given the importance of trap placement, and the great disparity in relative site advantage, it is not surprising that social regulation governs the dispositions and control of fixed facility sites. Certain strategic fishing sites are called *dehsuse:* each is named, and access to it is controlled. Fixed facilities are installed at these sites. The sites are considered the property of sib ancestors and are therefore in the custody of the senior sib member. He may allocate these sites on a usufruct basis or may retain his prerogative of priority access and organize the collective installation, maintenance, and harvest of the traps. Fish harvested from the regulated traps are to be shared by all village members in a communal meal.

One Wanano village is occupied by two sibs, a senior and a junior. The junior sib settled at the site prior to the senior sib's arrival and controlled all *dehsuse* sites. When the senior sib arrived, rights to these sites were transferred to them. Now all *dehsuse* sites are in the hands of the senior sib.

A second Wanano village is inhabited by a chiefly sib, Diani Pona, and a sib of servant status, the Wiroa. The "servant" sib has no trap sites. They rely upon the chiefly sib to share the fish caught at their sites.

Soma is a village of Wiroa associated with the chiefly sib at Yapima. They previously resided at Yapima, laboring for the senior sib, as other Wiroa currently do at Mo. The Wiroa challenged their seniors and threatened to leave their service altogether. To appease them, the seniors at Yapima gave the Wiroa utilization rights to one of their waterfalls, in return for a portion of harvested fish and continued assistance in labor-intensive projects, such as feast-giving. At Soma, the Wiroa headman regulates the traps and coordinates the capture; the entire sib participates in harvesting the weir.

Arrangements negotiated by paired chiefly/servant sibs illustrate how access to productive fishing sites is balanced by the obligations associated with control. All fish from these sites must be shared with community members. Days ideally begin with a communal fish meal to which each male contributes to his capacity. Because functioning traps change with water level, sibs with traps that function in one season will come to depend upon others during other periods. In the long run, those with the most strategic sites will supply those with less productive sites or without any sites.

Summary

This chapter on the Uaupés environment and resource utilization among the ranked Wanano sibs suggests the following summary statements:

1. Fishing productivity is highly variable over time and space.

2. Variation in productivity is patterned, permitting a degree of predictability and the development of specialized technologies.

3. Some locations are more productive than others, yielding a

greater fish biomass. Strategic sites provide access to the few habitats, such as rapids and flooded forests, where fish concentrate, or lend themselves to the installation of fixed fishing facilities.

4. All productive sites are controlled by corporate descent groups; access is subject to social control, generally on the basis of utilization rights associated with rank.

Chapter 8. The *Po?oa* Exchange

THE MEANINGS AND OBLIGATIONS associated with rank are nowhere better illustrated than in the system of reciprocal exchange known as the *po?oa*. I have briefly mentioned and will later consider in detail how redistribution operates on the local level: the chief, as senior member of a sib, controls productive sites. In this way, he maintains priority access to strategic resources, allocating them at his discretion to individuals in the local group. The chief thus fulfills his obligation to distribute food and at the same time manifests his "succulence."

When we draw back from the local sib to consider the more than fifteen distinct language groups inhabiting the Uaupés basin, the matter of redistribution becomes more complex. Locations in this area differ in productivity over the annual cycle, creating abundance or shortages during different seasons. A major exchange network links some 10,000 Indians in these groups, moving foodstuffs and manufactured goods among them. A ceremony of exchange between sibs—the *po?oa*—structures redistribution. It governs an exchange system of foodstuffs and specialized manufactured items.

In its orthodox form, the *po?oa* formalizes the exchange of material goods between wife-exchanging (affinal) sibs, who express their mutual gratitude and ongoing ties through ceremonial offerings. Informants speak of the *po?oa* as an essentially affinal ceremony; this view is supported by myths that represent the *po?oa* as an expression of wife exchange. However, in practice, the *po?oa* extends to sibs outside the affinal relationship, circulating goods among local groups related by affinal, patron/client, or kin ties.

This chapter first describes the affinal *po?oa* then contrasts it with transactions between parties without affinal alliances. Each variation entails significant alteration of the rules of exchange and bears on the relations between the exchanging parties.

Equivalencies

Three categories of goods may be exchanged in the *po'oa:* (1) specialized, manufactured items; (2) cooked animal (and fish) foods; and (3) raw fruits and vegetables. All exchanges are accompanied by the drinking of beer. With notable exceptions, the rules of *po'oa* call for the exchange of items that are in the same category and have the same rank and related value.

Exchange of Crafts

Each language group is the exclusive manufacturer of a product that it trades with its affines during *po'oa* ceremonies. The Wanano are the sole producers of the *wahpanio*, a strainer used in manioc processing. Various in-law groups produce other items: the Hohodene (Baniwa of the Aiarí River) are the only source for grater boards used to grate manioc tubers; the Tukano make wooden benches that shamans use in curing; the Desana produce the *balaio* baskets used for making manioc bread. The Makú are the exclusive producers of heavy-duty gardening baskets that all river Indians use to carry manioc tubers and firewood. Each of these is associated with a specific exchange value:

   1 grater board = 1 shaman's bench
   1 strainer = 1 *balaio* basket = 1 garden basket
   1 grater board = 1 shaman's bench or 6–8 strainers

Cooked Animal Exchange

Game and fish, the items traditionally exchanged between affinal groups or between forest and river Indian groups, have equivalent exchange value. Two other items are also included in this category: leaf cutter ant (*Atta sexdens*) queens, which are captured in large quantities in seasonal nuptial flights and are highly valued; and *ba'tí* fruit (*Erisma splendens stafleu*), produced by trees that mature slowly, bear fruit sporadically, and in any case are found in small numbers.

This category of exchangeable goods is intermediate between the manufactured "artifact" class and the raw or natural class. It includes natural products that are cooked before the exchange; the fish and game have been smoked, the ants have been roasted, and the *ba'ti* fruit boiled and fermented in the ground for many months. Small fishes are presented raw and are classified with raw fruits and vegetables.

Raw Fruit Exchange

This category includes all raw foods, most of which are forest fruits. Values and equivalencies of these goods are determined by a ranking system that orders the natural world, as the Wanano's designation of ranked brothers has ordered the social world.

Following the principle of hierarchical levels of inclusiveness that governs their social system, the Wanano distinguish "genus" and "species" levels of fruits. Each "genus" includes species that are ranked in relation to one another. For example, the category of fruit called *mené* (*Inga edulis*) consists of five "brothers"; the first is the sweetest and fleshiest; the others are said to be of decreasing succulence; the last is dry and infested with pests. The system is even more elaborate, for some genera are grouped into ordered classes and ranked in relation to the other genera within the class. *Mené* is grouped together with *toa* (Myrtaceae) and *wipí* (*assaí* in *língua geral, Euterpe oleraceae*); it is lower in rank than *toa* but higher than *wipí*. Some genera are considered equal in status, and thus in value, to other genera.

When a trade is negotiated, the fruits exchanged must be equivalent in rank and value. A first-ranked *mené* can only be exchanged for a first-ranked fruit of another type. The principle guiding the exchange of food—that only foods of equal value may be exchanged—parallels the ideology and practice of wife exchange.

The Affinal *Po?oa*

Balanced Reciprocity and Deferred Payment

Intermarrying sibs may transact symmetrical exchange with deferred payment. The transacting parties are of different social units, that is, of different descent group affiliation. They are always of different language groups and often reside far from one another. Language and location are manifestations of their differences. But, like the goods they exchange, the parties must be of equivalent rank relative to the order within their own language group.

The wife-receiving sib initiates the first round of exchange and fixes the timing of the ceremony. The headman, together with the groom's father, summons sib members together to announce the event. The sib members then work together for several days to prepare the offering. Each adult male is expected either to manufacture a utensil or to present enough food to fill a garden basket. All sib members give identical gifts. Preparations of such offerings necessitate tremendous increments of labor, far beyond the daily work required for subsistence. I observed one man devote 79 hours to fishing for such an occasion; two other observed fishermen spent 51 and 41.5 hours preparing for the same event.

The offering is expected to be substantial. Certain seasons, which bring rising waters or fruiting, make great surpluses available for short periods.[1] Donations often correspond to these circumstances.

When a commodity is available in sufficient quantity, the donor group gives the receiving group several days' notice of its intended presentation. Recipients are expected to ready themselves ritually for the event and to prepare beer for their donor-visitors. On the morning of the designated day, the donating group packs baskets of offerings into large canoes and travels to the recipient's village. On arrival, the donors place the gifts before the house and dance around them several times. Still dancing and playing flutes, they then carry the gifts into the precise center of the house.

The "owner" (*pütoro*) of the ceremony is the donor and visitor. As the gift-givers, he and his sib host the ceremony. At the same time, they are made welcome and offered beer; the recipient headman takes the lead in extending hospitality, as behooves a house-owner and sib "head."

Once the gift has been formally accepted and transferred, the recipients ask the donors to select the repayment. This negotiation is brief, for the donors have settled on a return gift before making their donation. While the timing of repayment is the prerogative of the repaying sib, the initiating donor determines both his initial payment and repayment. It is considered honorable to supply the exact gift requested; but it is also honorable (and practical) to request goods that the repaying sib can easily supply. Groups can and do negotiate if a demand cannot be met, but this is not usually necessary. The exchange follows a simple principle; each sib gives what the other sib does not have.

Where payments are deferred, ties are ongoing. Groups bound in alliance are continually receiving and owing. The assumption of contract and continuity underlies these relations. These groups are symbiotic in that they exchange wives. *Po꞉oa* ceremonies reinforce and represent this mutual interdependence. At the same time, they effect the timely transfer of goods from their place of origin, where they are abundant, to sites often some distance away where they are in short supply. Table 10 itemizes exchanges between Wanano and sibs with affinal ties.

Cases 1 through 4 are exchanges of meat for fish. Wife-givers provide the Wanano, who hunt but little, with meat. Gerardo Reichel-

Table 10. *Items Exchanged in Wanano* Po?oa *with Affines*

Affinal Group	Affine's Gift	Wanano Gift
1. Desana	meat	fish
2. Desana	meat	fish
3. Desana	meat	fish
4. Desana	meat	fish
5. Baniwa Hohodene	fish	fish
6. Desana	*balaio* baskets	strainers
7. Baniwa Hohodene	grater boards	palm fiber hammocks
8. Tukano	garden baskets	strainers
9. Tukano	*ba?tí*	fish
10. Baniwa Hohodene	fish	fish
11. Baniwa Hohodene	fish	awaiting payment

Dolmatoff (1971) has noted that the Desana symbolically equate fish with the female; this association may relate to the fact that the Desana, who hunt more than the Wanano, receive from their wife-givers the appropriate exchange for meat—fish. Wanano, on the other hand, are "fish-givers," never giving meat offerings. They receive meat from their in-law groups (wife-givers therefore = meat-givers), as well as from Makú (Peogü). The transaction satisfies the criterion of exchanging different goods of equal value by different descent groups of equal rank.

Cases 6, 7, and 8 are appropriate exchanges of specialized manufactured goods; each item is equivalent to, yet different from, the other. Case 8 is noteworthy, since the garden baskets offered by the Tukano in-laws had been made for them by a Makú group whom they consider to be their "clients" or "servants." This is a case of secondary or indirect exchange, where an item received in one *po?oa* is later exchanged in another.[2] Case 9, a trade of *ba?tí* fruit for fish, is yet another example of exchanging different items of equal rank.

In cases 5 and 10, fish was exchanged for fish. This satisfies the criterion of equivalent value, but appears to contradict the regulation of qualitative difference. But in each case, one type of fish was traded for another.

We have seen in previous discussions that the highest-ranked sibs usually control the most precious resources and that the highest-ranked sibs of different language groups intermarry. Since the flow of material goods through the conventional *po?oa* ceremony follows marriage lines, we may conclude that the highest-ranked groups in this way reinforce their access to preferred resources and productive sites.

Po꞉oa between Forest and River Indians

Immediate Balanced Reciprocity

The *po꞉oa* between affines or consanguines is characterized by payment over time. In contrast, in the *po꞉oa* between a river Indian group such as the Wanano and seminomadic forest groups, known as Peogü or Makú, payment is immediately balanced. No debits or credits are accrued; no ongoing relationship is presumed. In contrast to intermarrying riverine groups, the absolute separation of reproductive spheres divides forest and riverine groups; they do not seek one another's women. Their mutual relations are based, at least in part, on the desirability of material goods available in the other's locale. The Wanano receive game and garden baskets; the Makú receive cultivated products, particularly manioc flour and coca leaves.

The Wanano do not enter the forest for fear of dangerous forest spirits. The Makú avoid the river, believing river Indians to be powerful sorcerers who make them ill. Exchange occurs when a Makú band associates with a patron river group, with which it has established long-term relations. Among such patron river groups was the Desana in-law sib Simi Paro Pona residing among Wanano at Bucacopa. During the period in which the Makú visited their Desana patrons, many Wanano sibs, in-laws to the Desana, invited them to *po꞉oa* exchanges in order to obtain specialized Makú products— game and baskets.[3]

These transactions do not create or imply solidary relations between the Wanano and Makú: no single prestation presumes another. Every transaction is closed, stable, and final.

The Wanano and Makú reportedly negotiated the exchanges shown in table 11 between 1970 and 1974. The Wanano state that they initiate all exchanges with the Makú. However, since the Wanano do not enter the forest, the Makú obviously determine the timing and frequency of contacts. While the Wanano regard themselves (and other sedentary river Indians) as superior, the Makú largely control the circumstances of their transactions (Chernela 1983). The Makú apparently time their exchanges with the Wanano to correspond to the dry season, when animals clustering around the fewer available water sources facilitate game capture.

Table 11. *Items Exchanged in* Po?oa *among Wanano and Makú*

Wanano group	Wanano trade	Makú trade	Month
1. Biari	fish	meat	August
2. Nyapia	raw garden produce	meat	unknown
3. Nyapia	manioc flour	meat	unknown
4. Wekbea	fish	meat	August
5. Wekbea	fish	meat	August

The Agnatic *Po?oa*

Asymmetrical Reciprocity

The agnatic *po?oa* adheres to the ceremonial format of the affinal *po?oa*, but violates some of its basic conventions, including the rule of equivalency. This departure from the orthodox form of *po?oa* reflects the differing social interactions among agnates and affines.

In affinal exchanges, transacting parties of different language groups engage in symmetrical wife exchange. The affinal *po?oa* corresponds to the symmetry of the marriage exchange; exchanges between agnatic sibs, in contrast, lack symmetry. Equivalency cannot be the rule, since sibs of the same language group may never hold equal rank.

A basic difference between agnatic and affinal exchanges is the role played by hierarchy and status in the participating sibs. The differing ranks and corresponding expectations of the sibs inform agnatic exchange.

First I will discuss status behavior as it is manifested by initiation of exchange and visitation. Then I will turn to the issue of equivalence.

Initiative.   A junior agnatic sib wishing to initiate a *po?oa* need only approach its senior brother sib with the conventional overture: "We are hungry. We want to eat [named item]." Any sib without a food item is entitled to solicit it from a senior brother sib that has it. In this way, exchange between agnates may be petitioned by a junior sib, but the senior sib remains the formal initiator. The fact of the request is never formally acknowledged and does not diminish recognition of the donors' generosity. As in any other *po?oa*, the donor sib's prestige matches the abundance of the gift.

This practice contrasts with the affinal *po?oa*, in which the donor

Table 12. *Items Exchanged in* Po?oa *among Wanano Agnates*

Donor of higher rank	Donor of lower rank
1. *nyümü* (fruit)	no exchange
2. *ne?e* (fruit)	no exchange
3. *ba?tí* (fruit)	fish
4. raw fish	*pü* (fruit)
5. raw fish	*ne?e* (fruit)
6. *simi* (fruit)	no exchange
7. *pü* (fruit)	*ne?e* (fruit)
8. *nyümü* (fruit)	raw fish
9. *simi* (fruit)	raw fish
10. *mene* (fruit)	raw fish
11. manioc	*nyümü* (fruit)
12. ants	fish
13. *ne?e* (fruit)	*nyümü* (fruit)
14. raw fish	*toa* (fruit)
15. raw fish	*simi* (fruit)
16. *ne?e* (fruit)	raw fish
17. raw fish	small fish
18. manioc	no exchange

may control both the initial and the return payment. In the agnatic *po?oa*, the recipient often covertly controls the initial prestation. Control of the return payment hinges on rank, as discussed below.

Visitation. Whereas in the affinal *po?oa* the donor group always travels to the recipients' settlement as a sign of respect, in the agnatic *po?oa* the junior sib is obliged to visit the senior sib, regardless of donor or recipient roles. This accounts, in part, for the fact that downriver groups hold many more exchange ceremonies than upriver groups, as observed by Christine Hugh-Jones (1979).

Exchange Value. The more senior sib determines repayment and may subsequently find fault and demand correction. The range of variation in items exchanged is broader than in affinal exchange. Affinal exchanges must conform with the equivalences indicated above, to satisfy the Wanano expectation of balance. Trade between agnates seldom meets this standard, because the principle of rank and its associated obligations overrides the convention of equivalency. The principle of hierarchical brotherhood and the degree of generosity associated with each rank govern the value of items given and received. Table 12 reports goods exchanged in *po?oa* between agnates.

In terms of equivalency, the only agnatic exchanges that resemble affinal ones are case 3, in which *ba?tí* is exchanged for fish; and case 12, in which ants are exchanged for fish. The *ba?tí* fruit traded in case 3 did not originate in the donor village; the processed *ba?tí* had been obtained in an affinal *po?oa* with the highest-ranked Tukano sib, which lives on the Papurí River where *ba?tí* grows. This case demonstrates the movement of goods among in-law groups of equal rank by means of the affinal *po?oa* and redistribution from higher- to lower-ranked sibs by means of the agnatic *po?oa*.

Another form of reciprocal, balanced exchange between agnates involves forest fruits. In cases 7 and 13, two different forest fruits of equal value are traded. Typically, forest fruits mature, ripen, and fall within a very short period. Humans must compete with macaws, parrots, monkeys, tapirs, and other animals (including fishes) for these fruits as they ripen. The Wanano carefully watch the fruit, planning for harvesting and *po?oa* exchange. At the appropriate moment, the community collects large baskets full of these fruits and within one or two days distributes them to a brother group. Repayment is made when a different type of fruit matures near the exchanging village. For example, the palm fruits *ne?e* (mirití in *língua geral, Mauritia flexuosa*) and *nyümü* (*bacaba* in *língua geral, Oenocarpus bacaba*) are frequently exchanged. The first ripens in January, and the second in June.

An outstanding difference between the affinal and agnatic *po?oa* is the number of prestations for which counterpayments are imbalanced or nonexistent. In cases 1, 2, 6, and 18, high-ranked donating sibs refused repayment, claiming that their offerings were too modest in value to merit a return gift. The donation of a pure gift (follow-

Table 13. *Fruit Identification*

Wanano	Common Name*	Scientific Name
nyümü	bacaba	*Oenocarpus bacaba*
ne?e	mirití	*Mauritia flexuosa*
ba?tí	japurá	*Erisma splendens stafleu* (Vochysiaceae)
simi	wacu	*Macrolobium multijugum*
mene	ingá	*Inga edulis*
toa	uinapixuna	Myrtaceae

*In Portuguese or *língua geral.*

ing Malinowski's 1922 typology, p. 177) stresses the sentiment of brotherhood while aggrandizing the high-ranking group's generosity. Overpayment enhances the senior group's prestige and accentuates its status.

In several cases (4, 5, 14, 15, and 17), a highly valued food, fish, is exchanged for fruit or other less valued food. In case 4, a high-ranked sib in Yapima gives the fish auchinipterid and asks for fruit in exchange. This species of fish is found in flooded forest areas. The offering was made in May, when the riverbanks overflow and these fish are abundantly available in Yapima, the only Wanano settlement with access to flooded forests. During this high-water period few fishing methods are feasible, leaving flooded forests as the only viable fishing sites. The case illustrates the movement of goods from a locale with a temporary surplus to another in which the item is scarce. The donating sib was therefore the only possible supplier of these and possibly of any other fish during the high-water season. As chiefs they requested a repayment far below the value of the supplied item.

In cases 14, 15, and 17 the senior group initiated an exchange after solicitation by a junior group. As seniors, they asked for an item of lesser value in return.

Cases 8, 9, 10, and 16 would appear to depart from the pattern we have identified: the higher-ranked sib giving items of higher value. But in fact the pattern holds, for the fish exchanged were small and were offered in raw form. As noted, small, uncooked fish are included in the "raw" category and are equivalent to fruit in exchange value.

The exchanges of manioc are also of some interest. The plant parts presented are not the edible tubers, but, instead, the noded stalks from which the plant is reproduced. The bundles of manioc stalks presented to the receiving sib settlement include cultivars (subspecies) that they do not have. This gift choice is usually associated with starting a new garden, as when a couple has recently married.

Labor and Exchange. We have observed that, at least downriver, first-ranked sibs, known as chiefly sibs, are paired with "servant" or "slave" sibs, the Wiroa. The *po?oa* ceremonial requires intensive labor, particularly to process manioc and other fruits into beer.[4] The "servants" participate in the *po?oa* of the chiefly sib by preparing great quantities of beer and participating in the collection of items for exchange. The most senior Wanano sib, the Biari Pona, was associated with three client sibs, which greatly enhanced its capacity for demonstrating generosity in *po?oa* celebrations.

Discussion

Three types of economic relationships exist among the Wanano and find expression in the *po?oa* celebration:

1. Affinal relations: egalitarian, balanced, reciprocal.
2. River Indian/forest Indian relations: non-egalitarian, reciprocal, balanced.
3. Agnatic relations: hierarchical, redistributive, characterized by senior-to-junior offerings with partial repayment.

A fourth relation, head/tail, where head refers to "chiefly" groups and tail refers to "servant" groups, involves the exchange of resources for labor.

Affinal Exchanges

Affinal exchanges are based upon reciprocity. Items of equivalent value—either manufactured utensils or foodstuffs—are exchanged. These fall into three categories: specialized, manufactured utensils, which can only be obtained through marriage alliances; meat for fish, which can be obtained either through resource access (and increased production) or through access to procurers; and fruits in processed form.

The *po?oa* as it occurs among affines and between forest (Makú) and river Indians is clearly a reciprocal exchange. The exchange is always two-sided, involving gift and countergift, and always satisfies fixed criteria of equivalence. Exchange between affines reinforces mutual solidarity and ongoing relations. Each group determines the timing of its offering, seeking to make the most extravagant possible display. The wife-receiving group initiates the first round, determining both its payment and its repayment. In time, the situation will be reversed, with the other sib initiating a new round and repayment.

River/Forest Exchange

In *po?oa* between forest (Makú) Indians and river Indians, such as the Wanano, the transaction is immediate and presumes no ongoing relationship. The payments are balanced and completed in a single ceremony. The exchanges are always fish for game or manufactured for agricultural goods. The balance of value in the items exchanged sets on its head the conviction among Tukanoan river groups such as the Wanano that the Makú are unequals. Manufactured goods received in exchange with Makú can later be redistributed in affinal and agnatic exchanges.

Agnatic Exchanges

Po'oa exchanges between agnate groups follow a different set of principles and encompass a greater variety of exchange models. This departure from rigorously balanced reciprocity reflects the contextual and pragmatic character of the agnatic *po'oa*, setting it apart from the affinal. At its most solidary extreme, the agnatic *po'oa* includes the altruistic "pure gift," for which no return is expected. But it may also entail either balanced or symmetrical reciprocity or, in many cases, unbalanced, asymmetrical reciprocity. The agnatic *po'oa* merges the heuristic categories of reciprocity and redistribution. It reflects and reinforces the contrast between affines, who are different in terms of basic identity (i.e., descent affiliation) but equal in rank, and agnates, who are same in terms of descent affiliation but unequal in rank. Wife exchange links equally ranked sibs of different language groups; this interaction is followed and paralleled by an exchange of material goods. The ranks of wives and value of goods exchanged are expected to be equal. In contrast, the relationship among agnates builds upon a sentiment of brotherhood and common ancestry that carries the guarantee of economic cooperation.

If the *po'oa* is an affinal ceremony, as the Wanano perceive it to be, it may be seen as an affinal solution to a set of agnatic problems: unequal access to resources and social inequality among kin groups. The conventions of the *po'oa* conform with the principle that high rank implies obligatory generosity. In this way, the *po'oa* reduces potential conflict stemming from an unequal access to or distribution of resources.[5]

It has been argued that the potlatch exchange serves the function of equalizing potential differences in food and other resources of the Northwest Pacific Coast societies (Suttles 1960; Vayda 1961; Piddocke 1965). But this claim presents a number of problems. Potlatch assumes the ideal of the ultimate equality of all groups in terms of long-term access to resources. No explanation is offered for groups with fewer resources. Suttles concedes that such groups should presumably "drop out" of the system. This hardly lends support to an argument of "adaptation" or even of "equalization." Furthermore, given the practice of rank endogamy, an economic model allowing only for affinal, reciprocal exchange would lead to consolidation of resources and disequilibration. This is precluded by an institution-alized movement of goods among groups of different rank.

The Wanano case, which combines several types of exchange, con-forms with the claims of the idealized potlatch model, whereas ex-isting data from the Northwest Pacific Coast do not. In the Wanano system, the agnatic *po?oa* circulates goods among groups with dif-fering access to resources. Two features make this possible. First, junior agnate groups can solicit needed items from senior groups. Second, the criterion of balanced payment is relaxed in agnatic ex-change. The sentiment of kinship and the prestige associated with magnanimity compensate the senior sib for the lesser return.

In a system such as the potlatch exchange, a group might indeed fall "back" or "out" if incapable of competing with or reciprocating gifts received from other groups. Small or poorly situated groups would be particularly vulnerable. In the Wanano case, "servants" by definition are "without place." They assist in the *po?oas* of chiefly groups.

Through the *po?oa*, short-term deficiencies are resolved by a sys-tem allowing affines or agnates to defer repayment, borrowing on time. Long-term, sustained imbalances are resolved through perma-nent, institutionalized dependencies, one of which is the organiza-tion of rank and the structure of distribution from seniors to subor-dinate agnates.

Two processes are at work: one, consolidation through rank en-dogamy, by which groups with the highest rank exploit affinal (privi-leged access) exchange to consolidate the most abundant resources; and the other, the mechanism by which a group in need may ask any brother (agnate) group for a resource. The latter process undermines the former potential for consolidation, creating material egalitari-anism within an entity that is symbolically hierarchical. The first process guarantees the pedigree of rank; the second guarantees that through the incumbent obligations of rank the system is materially egalitarian. Exchange practices in this way dramatize the seeming paradox between hierarchy and egalitarianism and demonstrate that the terms "hierarchical" and "egalitarian" can both describe Wa-nano society.

PART IV: ORDINARY DRAMAS

Chapter 9. Rank and Leadership within a Wanano Settlement

TWO CRISES THAT OCCURRED during the course of my fieldwork served to dramatize the function of rank as an organizing principle of Wanano life. Both events involved the senior-junior relationship—the first within a sib, and the second between sibs. The first crisis, the subject of this chapter, sheds light on the Wanano concept of authority, the resulting leadership system, and the meaning of rank in these contexts. The second, treated in the next chapter, reveals the economic and political concepts underlying a sib's claim to the privileges of seniority.

Hierarchical relations within Wanano social structure can be reduced to the relationship older to younger (i.e., senior to junior). The "older" or senior has the right to "speak" or relegate by virtue of his proper social placement as "head" (*duhtiriro*, "commanding one" or "seated one"). Chiefly power derives from the mechanism of chiefly succession through a senior primogeniture line and illustrates the importance of ascription as a factor in local politics. While these privileges form the basis of the chief-subordinate relationship both within the local sib and between sibs, the rigorous restrictions on chiefly prerogatives and the considerable obligations attending chiefly stature restore a measure of balance to the relationship.

Two political forces oppose and countervail one another in a Wanano local group: the recognized authority of chiefs and the prerogative of subordinates to withhold services if they choose. Cooperation might be withheld, for example, if expectations of distribution are not met. The subordinates' means of political control point to other factors affecting local leadership. In short, local power is dispersed rather than consolidated.

During my stay in Curideri,[1] intervention on the part of mission workers resulted in the separation of the two key economic and political functions: labor mobilization and redistribution.[2] The results included a complete halt to labor, a sorcery threat, and finally the chief's single-handed, toilsome service to the community.

Missionary Contacts

European contact has proceeded intermittently in the Uaupés area since the eighteenth century (see chapters 2 and 3). The Indians of the Uaupés were subject to enslavement from the early eighteenth century; this practice culminated in the slave raids associated with the rising market for rubber from 1870 to 1912.

Salesian missionaries entered the upper Rio Negro basin in 1915, promising that their presence would curtail the activity of slavers. The order established missions on the Uaupés River at Taracua in 1924, at Iauaretê in 1929, and at Pari Cachoeira in 1945. The Indians chose to stave off the conquering and dividing power of the slavers by relying on the mission's protection. In this way, mutual interest promoted the Wanano-Salesian relationship. Aside from protection from the slavers, the Salesians furnished manufactured goods and medicine.

In turn, the Salesians hope to induce more production from the Wanano. A principal goal of Salesian missionaries in the Uaupés area has been to intensify agricultural labor, reorienting the economy from a subsistence to a cash-crop basis. This would link the Uaupés economy to larger market systems, eventually integrating the region into the national economy. Replacing traditional leaders with younger men schooled in the mission's ideas is one means of realizing this policy. Ideally, the younger mission-educated leader would motivate villagers to cultivate cash-crops and manufacture marketable products, such as modified traditional crafts. When the old chief of Curideri died, the missionaries attempted to install such a young man in his place. A crisis ensued.

The Wanano Concept of Authority

The chieftaincy or headmanship of any Wanano village is held by its highest-ranked male. His authority rests on his position as the senior living descendant of the founding ancestor of the local senior sib; he is the "oldest brother" in his generation, known as *mahsa wami*, "the people's oldest brother." He is also called *dahpu* or "head," a term that refers not only to his leadership role, but also to the anatomical head, which "leads," "organizes," and "speaks for" the human body. These functions of the anatomical head attach to the head of the Wanano village. More specifically, the term refers

to the head of the ancestral anaconda, from whose body the exogamous language groups of the Uaupés originated. The highest-ranked
male is also called *pütoro,* which has been translated as both "first"
and "chief." Here I refer to the highest-ranked male as *mahsa wami.*

Wanano chieftainship entails control over three major aspects of
village life: fishing resources, labor, and ritual. A *mahsa wami* must
hold sway over all three areas to lead effectively. Inability to harvest
and redistribute fish, for example, will make it difficult for the
mahsa wami to mobilize and coordinate labor. Control, then, implies the obligation to redistribute.

Fishing Resources

In every settlement, prime fishing sites are controlled by the senior
sib member. These sites are designated because weir traps installed
there are particularly productive in terms of yield per man-hour. The
mahsa wami may allocate these territories on a usufruct basis, or
he may retain his prerogative of priority access and organize the collective installation, maintenance, and harvest of the traps. Fish harvested from the regulated traps are shared by all village members in
communal meals. Whenever there is surplus fish, the chief is expected to assemble the community to eat. Shared meals are also
expected to precede any communal work.

Labor

The chief mobilizes and coordinates communal labor, carefully bal-
ancing collective projects against individual work such as gardening,
so that collective and individual labor do not conflict. I observed
several kinds of community projects in Wanano villages, including
the construction and maintenance of houses, the clearing and burn-
ing of gardens, and the intensive preparations for intersib *po?oa* exchange ceremonies.

Ritual and Language

The *mahsa wami* is the spokesman for the sib and the community.
He must command leadership etiquette, display diplomacy in representing his sib to outsiders, and receive visitors with graciousness
and eloquence. The *mahsa wami* receives and redistributes the gifts
presented by other chiefs at *po?oa* ceremonies held in the chief's
residence, a spacious dance house. His skillful display of oratory and
ritual language reflects on the entire sib and manifests high rank.

Among the possessions exchanged between groups is language, which holds special importance in the Uaupés. Received from ancestors, language is a key symbol of identity, uniting a named group. When two affinal groups come together, as they do to give or receive wives or to exchange goods at subsequent ceremonies, they are also seen as exchanging their distinct languages. Each group's *mahsa wami* presides over these sib interactions. During such ritual gatherings, the chief must perform the specialized litanies that only the seniors know. This knowledge is the patrimony of ancestral inheritance. The litanies belong to the sib, but only the chief, who personifies its "head," may perform them. The litanies are complex, and their correct performance requires elaborate training.

The Curideri Case

Missionary Intervention

The Wanano village of Curideri (Turtle Egg Village), with a population of approximately 80, is a five-day canoe trip from the large mission at Iauareté. Curideri is occupied by two sibs: the senior Macaw-Eye sib and the junior Opossum-Ear sib.

In 1975, the aged chief of Curideri, Bati Diani, died. His younger brother, Dahsiro, would traditionally have succeeded him; however, the Salesian fathers saw Bati Diani's death as an opportunity to exert their influence. A missionary arrived at Curideri and proposed as chief Pedro, a Portuguese-speaking member of the lower-ranked Opossum-Ear sib. Raised partly in São Gabriel, the governmental post at the outskirts of the Uaupés region, Pedro was closely acquainted with national values.

Dahsiro, the senior Macaw-Eye in line to become chief, was outraged. He openly challenged the missionary, threatening to go to Iauareté to tear down the Brazilian flagpole. In response, the missionary ordered an open election, with Pedro as one of several candidates. At the election, Dahsiro announced, "The chief will be my nephew, Edu." As the son of Dahsiro's deceased younger brother, Edu was a member of the Macaw-Eye, the higher-ranking sib at Curideri. He spoke some Portuguese, but had not been educated in the mission.

When the Salesian father called for a vote, Edu won; the lower-ranking sib had declined to vote, deferring to the higher-ranking sib's choice. The outcome suggested the strength of the traditional hierarchy.

After Edu won the election, it soon became clear that the power structure at Curideri was far from settled. People complained that Edu was not a satisfactory leader. The former chief, Bati Diani, was frequently eulogized and praised for the "succulence" he had exhibited by providing abundant fish, hosting many exchange dances to show the sib's prosperity and generosity, acquiring in return imported goods and specialized utensils for the community, representing the group eloquently with his memorable oratory, and receiving visitors graciously.

Unable to fulfill these obligations, Edu was said to be "dry." Edu had neither the desire nor the preparation to lead, but had accepted the role at his uncle's insistence. Without a dance house, without control over a productive fishing installation, he was not the sib head and therefore could not speak on behalf of the sib. As a result, Dahsiro was designated *mahsa wami* and assumed this role in greeting all visitors. Furthermore, Dahsiro held dances and communal meals in the large dance house that he had shared with his deceased brother, the previous chief. It began to appear that the election had been a ploy to placate the missionaries.

The crisis was not soon resolved, however. Over the next two years, the chieftaincy continued to be divided. As senior sib member, Dahsiro retained the ceremonial functions and prime resources of a chief; he held control of the principal weir and the dance house; he hosted dances and communal fish feasts. To appease the missionaries—who were mainly concerned with the allocation of labor—he relegated to Edu, his puppet, the unappealing executive function of organizing the villagers' labor.

Work Stoppage

Without the full spectrum of leadership roles, Edu did not have the leverage to compel villagers to follow his initiative. He planned numerous work projects, including the construction of a large canoe to facilitate trade of artifacts for manufactured goods with the missionaries. But, between 1978 and 1979, attendance at collective projects declined until only three people responded to Edu's calls to work—his own younger brother and two visiting client sons-in-law in service to the community. Edu was obliged to solicit people's participation in a house-by-house round of visits. At last, a sorcery threat and an overt breach of authority precipitated open confrontation between Edu and the villagers.

As tensions mounted, an in-law Baniwa shaman walked through

the jungle from the distant Aiarí River to advise Edu of a hallucinogenic vision. The shaman said that a near relative was planning to assassinate Edu through sorcery.

Two days later, Edu learned that a member of the lower-ranking Opossum-Ear sib had planned to lead villagers in an open challenge to his authority by thatching a roof at the moment when Edu had scheduled work on the trading canoe. The action was intended to be nonviolent but decisive disobedience. Edu heard of the conspiracy at the morning communal meal on the day the canoe was to be built.

In Wanano society, to shout, to address a complaint directly, or to show any emotion is considered not only inappropriate but shameful. As a consequence, the quiet is seldom broken. Conversation, although frequent, is kept at a discreet low pitch; facial expressions and gestures are deliberately understated.

Despite these conventions Edu broadcast his anger and fear at the communal meal. He shouted in a tremulous voice: "You didn't go through me! You didn't come to me first! None of you works. I work alone. Now one of you is going to kill me. I do not sleep with your wives. I am not the proper chief. I was made chief by the mission. You are telling me that I am not the real chief. Now one of you is going to kill me. I haven't slept with your wives."

A few days later, Edu called a meeting. Continuing in a similar vein, he told the villagers: "I have something important to tell you. One of you is wanting to put holes in me. One of you is wanting to give me poison. One of you is envious of the work that I am doing. But I am not speaking behind your backs and I am not sleeping with my relatives' women. I never go with other women for this reason: not to be poisoned, not to be killed. I am telling all of this to you. One of you wants to kill me. A shaman told me this."

The sorcery threat obviously worried Edu. It was a dramatic materialization of his greatest fear—a direct challenge to his role. Since the threat and the villagers' confrontation occurred within days of each other, it is difficult to say which, if either, incited Edu to action. In any case, he finally undertook an effective course of action, asserting his authority. He made the rounds of houses, sitting in each to make the appropriate ritualized but affectionate small talk. Furthermore, he announced that he was sponsoring a very large dance at which his son and other boys would receive life-breath names.

Then Edu set off on a fishing expedition that lasted four and a half days. When he returned in the evening of the fifth day, his wife smoked fish until the following morning. In the morning, she visited each household with offerings of fish. Villagers commented with approval; several said, "*This*, at last, was chief's behavior."

In contrast, Dahsiro was dour. He complained that if "everyone" held dances in his house, he would be exposed to menstruating women and other elements that pose danger to a shaman. Dahsiro, aside from being in line for the chieftaincy, also happened to be a powerful shaman. Nevertheless, Edu's naming ceremony—three days of uninterrupted hospitality—was considered a great success. In the weeks before I left Curideri, complaints about Edu had abated. On another visit several months later, I saw that Edu had expanded his house.

Though the power struggle between Dahsiro and Edu continued, the younger man had clearly established a measure of legitimacy. Ironically, while missionary intervention had hoisted him to chieftaincy, he began to assume that role in fact as well as in name only when he reverted to traditional styles of authority.

Implications of the Leadership Crisis

Missionaries in the Uaupés are attempting to shift authority from descent, its traditional locus, to a power configuration that has the mission as its authoritative and economic center. To this end, they introduce new status positions that undermine the hereditary basis of the chieftaincy and attempt to use their candidate for chief as a link between the village and the mission. The mediating chief is expected to encourage villagers to produce surplus agricultural products to be traded, on an individual basis, for manufactured goods at the mission.

At Curideri, the Wanano did not accept the authority of the individual chosen in the election instigated by the missionaries; nor did they agree to perform the export-driven tasks. In Wanano society, traditional authority is legitimized not by consensus, but by descent and concomitant control over redistribution. Rather than allow the mission to usurp the traditional power structure, the hereditary successor to the chieftaincy named a figurehead. In effect, the traditional system, with the hereditary successor as *mahsa wami*, went underground. The missionaries nevertheless viewed the figurehead as chief; they failed to see that the hereditary successor assumed leadership and all of its responsibilities, except mobilization of labor. The Wanano in this way resisted the challenge to their political integrity and retained the principle of chiefly succession within the primogeniture line.

Although the ruse deceived the missionaries and to some degree thwarted their goal, instability resulted due to the wrenching apart of the traditional *mahsa wami* functions: mobilizing labor, redistributing resources, and presiding over ritual. Partial resolution came only when the elected compromise chief asserted his legitimacy by fulfilling the chief's traditional obligations.

Several symbols demonstrate that the leadership system at Curideri, and indeed the Wanano concept of authority, remained intact despite Edu's election. First, Edu defends his limited authority by stating, "I do not sleep with your wives. I am not the proper chief. I was made chief." He makes these statements in the context of a plea to the villagers to forgive his incapacity to lead properly. In so doing, he hopes to communicate his political impotence so that sympathetic listeners will forgive him his wrongs. A traditional symbol of usurpation, the appropriation of others' wives, is denied. An agnatic dilemma—namely, chiefly succession within the sib—is inverted and expressed through a powerful sexual metaphor.

A second symbol shows that Edu worries about not only his power, but about his life. According to Marshall Sahlins, "Every chief acts as conqueror when he comes to power, Hawaiians say. And even if he has not actually killed his predecessor, he is presumed to have poisoned him" (1981:24). At first, Edu makes no effort to seize Dahsiro's power. All power bestowed upon Edu emanates from Dahsiro. He has not threatened or poisoned Dahsiro; rather, Edu learns from the Baniwa shaman that he himself is the target of an assassination plot. Again, a fundamental symbol of usurpation and power is inverted. "One of you is wanting to give me poison," Edu cries, fearing that his own authority and person are endangered. Communication of this threat by an in-law may also be seen as the result of Edu's agnatic dilemma.

Poison as a symbolic means of usurpation figures again in the episode when Edu asserts traditional authority, but now Edu is the poisoner. When Edu finally presides over a successful naming ceremony, a ritual previously in Dahsiro's province as *mahsa wami*, Dahsiro claims that Edu has brought him into the polluting presence of menstruating women. This exposure threatens his shamanic powers. With this poison—menstruating females—the pretender usurps his uncle's authority and symbolically reverses his former impotence.

Edu prevails, but legitimation of his chieftaincy hardly introduces the new system of leadership intended by the mission. Indeed, it represents a reassertion of the old. In his writings on "Deviance and Social Control," Robert Murphy writes about a Mundurucú chief who finds himself in much the same position as Edu:

The contemporary Mundurucú chief is in a dilemma. If we look upon a boundary role as one in which both ends have to be played against the middle, we see the chief caught between the interests of the trader and those of his followers; these interests rarely coincide. It is a difficult position, but one that can be maintained by maximal adherence to the traditional behavior expected of chiefs and minimal acquiescence to the demands of the traders. (1961:58)

After considerable difficulty, Edu learns to take the route of "maximal adherence to the traditional behavior expected of chiefs." Initially, he lacks the resources and knowledge to emulate the style of leadership that is traditional at Curideri. The period of upheaval tests Edu, forcing him to learn and then implement the traditional forms of authority and compelling him to acquire the resources needed to gain recognition as a leader.

Lacking control of a fixed fishing facility that might yield a substantial harvest with minimal labor, Edu resorts to strenuous, single-handed physical labor. The fishing trip satisfies the villagers' expectations. At the same time, it suggests the leverage of the work force, which can move chiefs to distribute goods by withholding labor.

Edu's dilemma was that, though a nominal chief, he could not be the "head" since he was not the highest-ranked sib member. The resulting disjuncture between "head" and chief is not customary in Wanano society; normally, as we have seen, the *mahsa wami* controls fishing resources, labor, and ritual. Because he was not "head," Edu could not for some time redistribute goods obtained from fishing and exchange ceremonies. He was, therefore, "dry."

The "succulence" that the past chief was said to have embodied might appear to be a personal attribute. However, this quality refers not to the person, but rather to the structure of redistribution. That is to say, "succulence" is the equivalent of maximal redistribution, and "dryness" the equivalent of minimal redistribution. In such a system, even charisma cannot replace redistributive capacity as a basis for leadership.

Conclusion

By presiding over the redistributive system of ritual exchange, the *mahsa wami* recycles surplus within the community and in this way undermines outsiders' efforts to accumulate surplus for export. When the young chief installed as a result of the mission's intervention reverts to traditional leadership behavior, he thereby defeats the purpose of his election.

In the final analysis, the mission failed in its attempt to become the center of economic and political action at Curideri. As Dahsiro's puppet, Edu could not induce labor so long as he could not fulfill other chiefly functions, including redistribution and hospitality. The case indicates that, unless he fulfills these expectations, a leader will not be recognized.

In summary, the Wanano tradition of redistribution prevents the accumulation of surplus goods for export. The mission's effort to change this practice by introducing a new leader was doomed to eventual failure, since only through redistribution will a leader's authority be recognized by the Wanano. However, this does not mean that the traditional system is invulnerable to external influence. In the next chapter we will see how the demise of the highest-ranking sib, brought about in large measure by migration, destabilizes relations within a Wanano settlement.

Chapter 10. The Bucacopa Case: Rank and Obligation among Three Uaupés Sibs

CHAPTER 4 DESCRIBES THE WANANO MODEL of social organization and demonstrates that rank is a feature of the descent system. Rank positions are theoretically inherited and fixed. However, one might expect departures from this model, for covert manipulation of status typifies rank systems. This occurs even in stratified societies, for example, in Polynesia (Goldman 1955, 1957).

The Bucacopa case documents one attempt at manipulation of status. A sib of former servant status seeks to usurp the status, inheritance, and associated privileges of its declining chiefly partner sib, without assuming the concomitant obligations. In response, a competing in-law sib impedes access to resources, and the sole remaining descendant of the declining chiefly sib supports their resistance to the status claim. The year during which I observed this maneuver represents a brief interval in an extremely drawn out process—a still image of players in the midst of a complex interaction. But the glimpse of the actors and their postures reveals important aspects of their interplay.

The Three Sibs

The Biari Pona

The flooded forests to the north and south of the Uaupés are rich in native *Hevea brasiliensis*, the tree bearing the marketable resin from which rubber is made. From 1870 to 1912 Uaupés Indians were removed from indigenous villages into rubber camps. With the temporary revival of world demand for Amazonian rubber during World War II, many Wanano were once again enticed by the promise of wages or carried by force to labor in rubber camps. Numerous men and women emigrated to rubber areas in this period. Once in the camps, many died of disease; others settled permanently in cities.

In the 1970s and 1980s the lure to earn wages in the cocaine fields of Colombia had the same depopulating consequences.

The site at Bucacopa housed the highest-ranked Wanano sib, the Biari Pona. By 1977 no Biari males were left at Bucacopa. A single Biari Pona(iro), a woman, was alive. She remained at Bucacopa with her Desana husband and her two Desana sons. With no male Biari Pona, the sib name could not be carried on; it was dead.

The Biari Pona sib had occupied the area of Bucacopa's large waterfall for as long as any informant could recall. Biari, the founding ancestor, was said to have been a powerful shaman. According to the Biari Pona's ancestral myth, Biari donned full shamanic regalia and used his shamanic powers to lower himself into the ground while seated on his shaman's stool. The myth tells that only Biari's head, which was transformed into stone, remained above ground. The sacred boulder at Bucacopa is said to be Biari's transformed head, a sign of his preeminence as a powerful ancestor whose authority still prevails at Bucacopa. The head as a symbol of authority is a common Wanano motif.

As the Biari Pona decline, two co-residing sibs, one in-law (Desana) and one agnatic (Wari Yuturia), make claims to Bucacopa and its strategic resources. The Biari Pona apparently believed that the precipitous decline in their numbers was the work of sorcerers of their co-residing servant sib, the Wari Yuturia, who may have envied their prosperity. The Biari Pona's conviction that they were envied implies that the high-ranked Biari had not been fulfilling their role as generous donors of resources. Redistribution theoretically precludes accumulation and should diminish envy. The Biari Pona's accusations of being the victims of witchcraft were apparently rooted in their knowledge that their failure to provide would undermine recognition of their status.

The Desana Sib

The Desana sib Simi Paro Pona maintains an ongoing marriage alliance with the Biari and moved to Bucacopa several generations ago,[1] at the invitation of the Biari. This is perhaps the only known case of exogamous moieties speaking different languages in the same location. The last remaining member of the Biari Pona sib, and consequently the highest-ranked living Wanano, is a woman named Nicho. Her husband is a Desana, and therefore her children are members not of the Biari sib, but of the Desana sib. Despite their long residence at Bucacopa, their importance as providers of Biari spouses, and their tie to the last remaining Biari, the Desana are still considered "visitors" or "mixers" (although they merit a specialized, in-law visitor status). They have no legitimate authority at Bucacopa. The Desana consist of two elderly brothers, their children (one of whom is Nicho's husband), and their grandchildren.

The Wari Yuturia

The Wari Yuturia, a sib related agnatically to the Biari Pona, had lived in a subordinate relationship to the higher-ranked sib for some time. While this relationship held, the Biari Pona provided the Wari Yuturia with fish from the large platform weir they controlled and in this way fulfilled the obligation associated with their status. The Wari Yuturia in turn rendered services related to their status as a servant group, such as assisting the Biari in annual construction of the large weir and in processing beer or collecting offerings for the large po?oa celebrations that the Biari Pona, as a sib of first rank and the "true heads" of the Wanano, were obliged to give. A Makú sib that left Bucacopa several years before my arrival had also resided seasonally at Bucacopa and assisted the Biari in the preparations for these festivities.[2]

The Conflict

Chiefly sibs normally have assisting servant sibs in their settlements. The Biari Pona at Bucacopa were the only sib to have three assisting groups: a client in-law sib, a servant sib, and a Makú sib. With the Biari's decline and the departure of the Makú sib, the two remaining sibs—the Desana and the Wari Yuturia—remained to lay claim to the Biari sib's resources and privileges. The dispute developed into open, violent conflict over control of the weir. This occurred during my stay in the neighboring Soma and Yapima villages in 1979, when the Wari Yuturia attempted to take control of Bucacopa's large communal platform weir.

In the absence of Biari males, the Desana had used Nicho's authority to maintain and harvest the large weir at Bucacopa. However, the Desana had no obligations to the Wari Yuturia in terms of generous redistribution; in turn, the Wari Yuturia were neither obliged nor willing to acknowledge the authority of the Desana. The Wari Yuturia presumably believed that only by controlling Bucacopa's strategic resources would they receive sufficient yield. A power struggle ensued, developing into violent conflict.

Nicho's sons—who are members of the Desana sib Simi Paro Pona—went to the Wari Yuturia when the takeover occurred, claiming to speak on her behalf. They warned the Wari Yuturia that, from Nicho's viewpoint, they were trespassing. As we will see, the dispute resulted in Nicho's departure from Bucacopa.

In contrast to the Desana, the Wari Yuturia base their claim on rank. They demand not simply utilization rights, but recognition as members of a subgroup of the Biari Pona. They state that their sib is, in terms of descent, one of the "Firsts," rather than one of the "Lasts"; in this way they lay claim to the rights associated with descent position. They have incorporated the Biari name into their own, becoming the Wari Yuturia Biari Pona.

The process of breakdown throws into relief Wanano expectations of how their structure is supposed to function. In this instance, social disorganization is met with efforts at both manipulation and creativity. The parties in conflict with each other operate within the same rule system, but each uses the rules to justify opposite ends.

Nicho: The Last Remaining Biari

At the outbreak of the dispute, Nicho became ill. Convinced of her impending death at the hands of powerful Wari Yuturia sorcerers, she left Bucacopa with her husband and sons to consult the powerful Fish-Eye (Wekbea Pona) shaman at Yapima. The Fish-Eye shaman exorcized two disease-causing substances from her forehead at a curing ceremony I attended. But he told her that a remaining third substance was difficult to retrieve. Chanting, shaking the shaman's rattle, and smoking tobacco, he called upon his supernatural Vulture assistant to provide insight. When at last he told Nicho that he perceived the source of her illness, he spoke with gravity and she fell to the ground sobbing. He said that he had seen a man smoking a long, powerful cigar and pronouncing incantations. He then said that Nicho's chances of survival were slight, since her relentless opponent would smoke until her death. The shaman advised Nicho to remain at Yapima.

In despair, Nicho dictated and sent letters to émigré Biari—sons of members of her father's generation who had emigrated to Colombian cities to secure wage labor in 1942, when the demand for rubber gatherers surged as a result of World War II. She invited their sons, who had been born in Colombia, to return to Bucacopa in order to retain Biari Pona control of the site. Nicho's letters to the nephews she has never met say that she is dying, and they must return home immediately. Her effort dramatizes the fact that descent, not residence, determines a sib's rights. Nicho considers the return of the diaspora Biari to be her last hope.

While at Yapima, Nicho sang a song to a "younger brother," a fellow Wanano of a junior sib. This personal lyric, which is presented later in this chapter, does not address directly the dynamics of the power struggle played out at Bucacopa, but expresses the grief of recent exile and of the sib's imminent extinction.

Implications of the Dispute

The Ideology of Rank, Control of Resources, and Redistribution

The Bucacopa case dramatizes the relationship of social organization, control of resources, and legitimate succession among the Wanano. The Wanano do not recognize individual ownership of property; a river section or weir site, for example, is "owned" by an ancestor and is not transferable. We may therefore speak only of "effective control" or "use rights," which accrue through patrilineal inheritance from a founding ancestor. Use rights are limited by kinship-phrased rules, according to which a sib's highest-ranked member administers its holdings. Use rights, morever, are accompanied by obligations—also phrased in terms of descent criteria—binding the distributor and recipient.

In the case of Bucacopa, the relations of a co-residing chiefly sib (the Biari), a servant sib (the Wari Yuturia), and an affinal sib (the Desana Simi Paro) break down as the chiefly sib nears extinction. Both the servant sib and the affinal sib reside at Bucacopa "by invitation"—that is, their presence was sanctioned by the Biari Pona, descendants of the founder. The Biari Pona and Bucacopa had been inextricably linked. The death of the Biari Pona's last male descendant ruptured the established order and created a management crisis. Complicating matters further is the unresolved issue of the status of the Wanano Wari Yuturia. That the "servant" sib resides at Bucacopa by invitation might have been allegation, not fact—one of the representations through which complementary relations between a chiefly and servant sib find expression.

Because property is collectively owned and administered by the senior living sib member, no one living within or without the sib may exploit Bucacopa's resources without the senior's authorization. But now there is no man in Bucacopa to act as rightful custodian of the resources or to fulfill the obligations associated with the role. And because land is not transferable, Nicho herself is not free to dispose of Bucacopa.

Nicho's ambiguous status isolates her. As a female, she has few rights; as a Biari, she does have rights that entitle her to authorize the use of the weir by the Desana. Her authority ultimately proves insufficient. For although it is said that her high rank makes her "like a man" and that "no one can call her younger sister," she does not possess the masculine prerogative of producing Biari offspring. Her children are eligible spouses for Biari offspring, essential for the group's continuity, but that is all. And there remain no Biari males for her future daughters to marry.

The sib vanishes, then, with the death of its founder's last male descendant. For the Biari, this has already occurred. With the sib's dissolution go all its rights and obligations. Convinced Nicho is to die, the Fish-Eye shaman counsels her to leave Bucacopa. Underlying his advice may be the belief that Nicho's existence is irrelevant: as a female she cannot maintain the rightful place of the Biari at Bucacopa.

Meanwhile, none of the other twenty-five Wanano sibs interferes. Theoretically, no other sib of any rank may occupy Bucacopa by right, since land cannot be transferred. In the absence of the ancestor's descendants, the situation is a legal stalemate.

The extinction of the Biari sib therefore creates a vacuum in the system, throwing into question the use of the Bucacopa territories by any sib. The Desana in-laws and the Wari Yuturia servants both lay claim to the facilities, rights, and territory of Bucacopa. Their stances in the dispute involve even greater ironies and legal contradictions and illuminate Wanano attitudes toward legitimacy and responsibility.

The only claim the Desana have to Bucacopa is their tie to Nicho, whose husband and sons are Desana. Nicho does not recognize the authority of the Wari Yuturia in the weir dispute and considers them impostors; she supports the Desana right to control the weir.[3] Although she believes that neither group has legitimate rights to Bucacopa, she backs the Desana—the non-Wanano sib, as opposed to the Wari Yuturia—the Wanano sib.

Each side denies the other's claim to rights. But if the servant group can convince the others of their legitimate place in the Biari rank system, they may then remain at Bucacopa with full rights.

The high-ranked Wanano sibs can resolve the dispute in several ways. They might bestow on the Wari Yuturia use rights without rank status. However, without rank there is no obligation to distribute fish or other resources that the Biari had been obliged to supply. The Wari Yuturia at Bucacopa might presumably reduce their production in this case.

Alternately, the first Wanano sibs might recognize the rank claims of the Wari Yuturia. In this case, they would receive the benefits of obligatory distribution. But would the Wari Yuturia have the proper ritual and mythico-historical inventory to legitimize their rank claims?

In practical terms, recognition of the Wari Yuturia as Biari Pona might cause the least upheaval. But Nicho, the only remaining Biari, contests their claim. Sympathy with the Wari Yuturia might lead to perpetuation of her sib; but the Biari Pona remains too present a reality for Nicho. She insists that her line represents the only legitimate Biari Pona.

The Wari Yuturia have not merely alleged the right to administer the weir—they have usurped it. By preparing and harvesting the weir alone, they have asserted more control than they have ever assumed in the past. Why did they choose to secure their claim by force? Nicho suggests their rationale: her song intimates that the dispute over the weir and the resulting sorcery originated in conflict over the inadequate distribution of Biari resources.

As we might expect, Nicho argues that her sib always complied diligently with their distribution obligations. In her song she cites her sister to testify to her magnanimity. The sister sings that Nicho was a generous provider of fish with pepper-water and manioc drink. She expresses dismay at the Wari Yuturia's envy: the Biari Pona's generosity should have precluded envy.

The issue of rights and obligations is two-sided. Members of junior sibs are expected to respect their senior brothers, even as members of senior sibs are expected to manage sib resources in the interests of the junior brothers. In the absence of Biari males, no descendants remained to concern themselves with the welfare of the Wari Yuturia. The remaining Biari female, Nicho, had been invoked by the Desana to legitimize their use of the weir at Bucacopa and to restrict the Wari Yuturia's access. But, unlike the Biari, the Desana are under no obligation to protect the interests of the Wari Yuturia. Frustrated by this state of affairs, the Wari Yuturia challenged the Desana authority, then forcibly seized the weir.

Social Disintegration of Tribal Hierarchies

Relative claims of the disputants aside, the Bucacopa situation exemplifies the wider contemporary problem of social disintegration among traditional tribal hierarchies. The disputing parties seek to manipulate sib order, but ideology dictates that sib order is fixed. In large part, the problems stem from decimation of groups of Indians as a result of contact with whites.

Along the Papurí River, for example, there are numerous sites belonging to extinct sibs. The present residents of those sites are thought of as temporary occupants, not as rightful owners. The extinct sibs are recalled by their brother sibs; the locales are maintained in both the geographic and social sense. The permanent Wanano sib order includes several extinct sibs. Informants report that the order never changes. Ideally, the order remains stable since it must meet certain mathematical requirements. Sib classes, for example, are composed of five or ten sibs—therefore, they are not easily accessible to manipulation. The site of the extinct Kenei sib, on the Uaupés river, is now occupied by a Cubeo community, said to be "visiting" by the Wanano. There is no challenge to Cubeo occupation of the site, yet the Wanano consider the site to belong to the extinct Wanano sib. Similar demographic erosion is the likely outcome of the conflict at Bucacopa. Whether the "visiting" Desana or the "servant" Wari Yuturia prevail, the site will still be thought of as belonging to the Biari Pona.

The growth or dissolution of sibs results from demographic fluctuations. A junior sib may exploit the decline of a senior descent line to usurp its position. Such is the case at Bucacopa.

Despite the efforts of the last remaining Biari to block the Wari Yuturia assumption of the Biari status, no other Wanano group has moved to prevent it. When Nicho flees to Yapima to consult with the next highest Wanano sib, she is advised to leave Bucacopa. This counsel indicates either tacit complicity with the upwardly mobile Wari Yuturia or a conviction of powerlessness.

Nicho's Song

At Yapima, Nicho sings a song that is excerpted below. Fear and grief inform the performance. She compares her existence in exile, away from Bucacopa, to that of a horsefly (14, 30) without a resting place. Her sense of disappointment broadens to include the historical displacement and eventual extinction of her people. In her lament, she assumes the voices of various individuals. Singing in the voice of her son, she prophesies that she will disappear like a piece of kindling wood. She has become "one who mixes" (27), meaning that she is neither where she belongs nor among the people with whom she belongs. She is "passing through" the village of her younger brothers, the Yahuri Pona, and "dragging her offspring with her" (11).

Nicho's First Song
> . . . Alone I am
> I have no brothers,

I go
Sadly
Here, where the river widens at Badia Kusu
And there, at the stream of the *tucunaré* fish.
There, upriver,
On the branch of a tree
Like a bird that goes
(10) Here and there,
Dragging her offspring with her,
Sons, who are Other people,
Says my oldest son . . .
"Like a horsefly
With its eyes plucked out
You fly hither and yon
Alone,
Because you are alone,"
He says . . .
(20) "And like a horsefly with its eyes plucked out
Batting about
You will do the same . . .
There, in Badia Kusu, on top of a tree branch,
There my mother comes flying with me,"
Says my son.

Nicho's Second Song[4]
I am one who drifts;
I am one who mixes.
I am moving among your brothers
And I haven't even one brother.
(30) Like a horsefly
That flies forward and backward
That flies here and that flies there,
"I am not like him," says my son, Dito?ano . . .
   [referring to the relative to whom she is singing],
I, yes, am granddaughter of the Biari ones . . .
"My *ingá* fruits are succulent with juices. . . ."
Biari woman,
That wanders in your midst
I am a person
(40) Raised on the bones of big fishes.
I am the daughter of one who spoke loudly, loudly.
I am a Biari woman.
". . . My mother has not even one brother . . .

She will disappear
Like a piece of kindling wood,
An ember that blazed momentarily,
Then turned to ash; my mother,
My mother that has no brothers . . .
I yes, I am the only son, my mother," says my son,
(50)   "I was grandson of Simi Paro Ponairo,
But they were a fine people!
Dianumio was my uncle!
But as they are no longer listening to these things,
All is sad, all is heartache and loss . . ." says my son.
After the deaths of my brothers
I am going, going . . .
My grandfather, yes, he said to me,
"My grandchild, my grandchild,
I leave you in my place
(60)   In my last moments."
He said to me, my mother, also,
"In my last hours, I leave you in my place."
I am, yes, I am
The Dianumia Nicho,
I am granddaughter of those who spoke loudly, loudly,
Wife of a Desana, and you cannot tolerate me . . .
I am daughter . . . of the Firsts,
Daughter of my Fathers,
Born of them, I am she.
(70)   My uncles sucked on bones, and tossed them out
And on those bones I sucked and on those bones I grew.
Now you also pass through. Pass!
You will see how it is
". . . There are some whose rage at our people,"
So they tell me,
Will poison and consume us. . . .
After I die in the homeland of our brothers
You will sing and leave remembrances.

Nicho continues to sing in the words of her deceased sister to
her son:
(80)   My in-law,[5]
Even as I die
I remember,
In my house

I gave to all:
A calabash of drink
And fish with pepper.
I gave, my in-law,
Even so . . .
When you arrive in my village,
(90)   After two or three days,
You will cry.

Discussion

The highest-ranked living Wanano, Nicho sings:

I am daughter . . . of the Firsts,
Daughter of my Fathers,
Born of them, I am she.
My uncles sucked on bones, and tossed them out
And on those bones I sucked and on those bones I grew . . .

Her words recall the Biari prosperity at Bucacopa, associating that abundance with their elevated rank. Again alluding to rank, and speaking now in the persona of her son, she sings: "My *ingá* fruits are succulent with juices" (36). Eloquence implies high status; similarly, the succulence of the *ingá* fruit implies rank, since foods in the Wanano view, like sibs and people, are ranked, first-ranked fruit being the most juicy.

Touching on a delicate social issue, the sorcery Nicho presumes to be aimed at her sib, she assumes the persona of her dead sister:

". . . There are some whose rage at our people,"
So they tell me,
will poison and consume us. . . . (74–76)

Nicho repudiates charges against the Biari Pona, recalling her sib's past generosity:

Even as I die
I remember,
In my house
I gave to all:
A calabash of drink
And fish with pepper. (81–86)

Nicho laments that the memory of the Biari Pona, and of their generous offerings to other sibs, has not been revered and argues that history provides no basis for envy. Underlying her words is the assumption that the demise of the Biari Pona stems directly from the sib's resource access and obligatory generosity.

Nicho's references to location, to placement in time and space, reflect her understanding of her position in the social order. As the last remaining member of her sib, she is without "even one brother" (29) at Bucacopa. She sings that she is "Like a horsefly / That flies forward and backward / That flies here and that flies there . . ." (30–32). Nicho has left Bucacopa: in a literal sense, this flitting about is spatial. But Nicho's predicament suggests a figurative meaning; she flies "here and there," "forward and backward" in time, in an attempt to link her ancestry to future generations. The futility of that effort is expressed when Nicho says, in the voice of her son, that "my mother has not even one brother . . . she will disappear / like a piece of kindling wood, / an ember that blazed momentarily, / then turned to ash" (43–47). The premonition of nonexistence is not only a spatial notion—decomposition—but also a temporal image—a break with the past.

Nicho dramatizes her loss of rank when she sings that not only will she lose her link with the past; her son is also displaced. The narrative shift from her own voice to her son's allows her to anticipate her own downfall, to foretell her son's agony without forfeiting dignity.

Nicho's narrative, like the horsefly, moves forward and backward, a generation forward and then a generation backward. In first her own voice, then the persona of her son, later the words of her father in the voice of her son, and lastly returning to her own voice she sings:

My grandfather, yes, he said to me,
"My grandchild, my grandchild,
I leave you in my place
In my last moments."
He said to me, my mother, also,
"In my last hours, I leave you in my place."
I am, yes, I am
The Dianumia Nicho. (57–64)

One generation, then, addresses a future generation in the voice of a past generation that states: "I leave you in my place." This is Nicho's most powerful image of diachronic placement. The grandfather's statement "I leave you in my place" is followed by the affirmation, "I am, yes, I am the Dianumia Nicho," involving her ancestral name. Nicho's ancestor placed her in order that she could exist ("I am, yes, I am"); but now she has lost that position and faces the dilemma of social nonexistence.

Nicho's narrative shifts express her consciousness of changed status, from that of a belonging one to that of a displaced one. Her statement, from her father's viewpoint, that "I leave you in my place," indicates that there had once been a place for Nicho, as the "granddaughter of those who spoke loudly" (65). This sense of belonging, which emanates from temporal links, connects Nicho to her father and his fathers. But now that Nicho does not belong, she realizes the implication for her son.

Nicho's desolation is intensified in that, as a wanderer, she carries the fate of her progeny with her. She characterizes herself in another song as "a bird that goes / here and there, / dragging her offspring with her" (9–11). Her son, like her, becomes "Other people" (12)— one of those who do not belong. Not only does Nicho fly from here to there, she cannot even see what lies ahead for her but, "like a horsefly with its eyes plucked out" (14, 15, 20), thrashes blindly about, threatened by unseen obstacles.

Chapter 11. Conclusion

LITTLE ATTENTION HAS BEEN PAID to societies that are neither stratified nor egalitarian. These societies have fallen through the mesh-
work of most classification schemes and most theoretical discussions of social inequality. Yet these very societies are diagnostic for
our understanding of hierarchy.

This work has examined a Native American society in the Northwest Amazon, with particular attention to its bounded descent
groups and ascribed social statuses. In Wanano terms, these amount
to vertical and horizontal "placements." The book takes this system
of placement, or social positioning, as its central theme.

Structure and Society

Descent

In Wanano society cross-cutting principles of common ancestry or
descent, on the one hand, and marriage, on the other, link individuals within and across descent groups. We have seen how relations
within the descent group are governed by kinship and characterized, in the socially specific sense defined here, by dominance and
subordination.

The metaphor of siblingship unites agnatic groups at every level;
seniority differentiates them, so that every individual within a sib,
and every sib within a language group, stands in a fixed rank relationship to every other. The exchange of names replicates the order
of seniority in each succeeding generation.

Each sib owns a set of exclusive ancestral names. Social distinctions, histories, and affiliations are maintained through sib names.
A first-born offspring takes the name of his grandfather, who took
the name of *his* grandfather, and so on. Later-born sons may take
any of the names belonging to the ancestral grandfather's younger

brothers. As siblings, ancestral and living, are always ranked according to seniority, so are the names themselves, each carrying an inherent, and invariant, connotation of rank. Thus, a chief, the first-born (of the first-born, etc.) of the ancestral First-Born, receives a First-Born name and thereby establishes his position in the hierarchy. Rank, then, is a language of social relations in which brotherhood and fatherhood are expressions of group membership and placement in relation to others.

Myth and Descent

The hierarchical basis for the relations among localized descent groups and their proprietary rights to particular locations derives from a charter myth relating the origins of all Eastern Tukanoan groups in the Uaupés. In this myth, a sacred anaconda canoe originates from a primordial Water Door and swims upriver to the region of the Uaupés River.[1] Reaching the headwaters, the anaconda canoe turns round, so that its head faces downriver and its tail upriver. From its body emerge brothers, progenitors of all of the sibs of the Uaupés. The birth order of sibs from the body of the ancestor becomes an order of status fixing the relations among sibs of a single language group. The highest-ranked groups are the first to emerge; they are born of the head of the anaconda. Succeedingly junior brothers emerge later, further upriver. The last, or lowest in rank, are born from the tail of the anaconda. The location at which each ancestor is said to emerge is known as the "sitting place" (*duhinia*), or the "topos" of that ancestor. Seatedness implies timelessness, as seated ancestor is incorporated into seated descendant by means of ritual "sitting-breathing." The term *makariro*, "one who belongs," conveys the Wanano ideal of permanence in time and space. The emergence of the ancestral anaconda from the river provides each ancestor's descendants with "place" and "past," constructing the proper "sitting-being," then, of each Wanano descent group.

The anaconda of the Tukanoan myth differs from other generative symbols, such as the Mediterranean ouroboros, portrayed as a snake with its tail in its mouth, for in the case of the Uaupés anaconda direction is its importance. Positioning is crucial, with tail and head seen as opposites, differentially weighted, and separated by a sequential ordering. The body of the anaconda thus establishes the relations of spatial orientation, descent, and hierarchy.

The myth of the anaconda establishes the river as a cultural topography, a mapping of social identities. It is a channel of connectivities as well as a marker of distinctions and boundaries between local descent groups. Anaconda *qua* river is the source of all legitimacy, integrity, and order.

Ritual

Rank is dramatized in the ceremonious distributional exchanges known as the *po?oa*. The *po?oa* constitutes a two-part exchange in which localized sibs offer and counteroffer gifts of specialized foods or crafts. When two Wanano sibs exchange items, the gift of the senior sib is expected to be greater in quality and quantity than that of the junior. The principle of hierarchical brotherhood and the degree of generosity associated with each rank govern the value of items given and received. The imbalance of the exchange establishes a difference that creates value; that value is rank. Each ritual exchange constitutes a means through which the social system is communicated and the social contract reaffirmed. Whatever power is associated with rank is derived from and generated in its exercise: you are what you give.

The role of chief is ideologically linked to generous behavior; he "gives" rather than "keeps." In order to manifest such generosity, he must be able to mobilize labor (generally subordinate affiliates) and resources to sponsor the prestations that enhance his own prestige and that of his affiliates. In the Wanano case, high rank is associated with "succulence" and expressed through redistribution. Succulence is the substantial exchange within which relationships are fixed and related identities are organized hierarchically.

Those who are high in rank are also linked ideologically to the more strategic resource areas; the increase in output that high-ranked groups require to display abundance is made possible both by their priority access to the most strategic resources and by their accumulation not of resources, nor of wealth, but of affiliating labor.

Through the *po?oa*, short-term deficiencies may be resolved by deferred repayment, borrowing on time. Long-term, sustained imbalances are resolved through permanent institutionalized dependencies, one of which is the organization of rank, and the structure of distribution from seniors to subordinate agnates.

Affinity

Cross-cutting this system of fraternal, hierarchically organized sibs are the ties produced by ongoing affinities, marriages over generations between cross-cousins of sibs of different language groups.

The proper transaction across language group boundaries is exchange. Language, women, and crafts are objects of exchange: the first through dialogue, the second through marriage, the third through the ritual *po?oa*. Each exchange is both a marker of differentiation and an agent of articulation. It may be further said that each of these exchanges stands for the other, so that dialogic exchange or gift exchange between speakers of two different language groups stands for the marriage exchange and is therefore a quintessential social transaction.

A basic difference between agnatic and affinal exchanges is the role played by status in the participating sibs of the same language group, where the differing ranks of the brother sibs are foregrounded and corresponding expectations related to rank inform each exchange.

Whereas the exchanges between agnatic sibs lack symmetry, exchanges between affinal sibs are characterized by value symmetry. Difference in kind, but equivalency in value, is the rule. The parties in affinal exchanges are wife-exchanging sibs of different language groups; the items exchanged in the affinal *po?oa* correspond to the symmetry of the marriage exchange.

Two processes are at work: one, the tendency of consolidation through rank endogamy, by which groups with high rank exploit affinal links and privileged access to consolidate the most abundant resources; and the other, the mechanism by which a group in need may ask any brother (agnate) group for a resource. The latter process undermines the former potential for consolidation, creating material egalitarianism within an entity that is symbolically hierarchical. The first process guarantees the pedigree of rank; the second guarantees that, through the incumbent obligations of rank, the system is materially egalitarian. Exchange practices in this way dramatize the seeming paradox between hierarchy and egalitarianism and demonstrate that the terms "hierarchical" and "egalitarian" can both describe Wanano society.

Despite an ideology that associates the notion of first with leadership, high-ranked leaders or groups have no coercive mechanisms with which to compel others to labor or to military action. This fundamental feature distinguishes ranked from stratified societies. Instead, high-ranked groups are dependent upon the labor of the low in rank in order to redistribute. High-ranked groups, must, in fact, compete to attract labor. The European concept of dominance, derived from warfare, is fundamentally different. The image of dominance, here, is succulence.

Models and History

In *The Dialectics of Social Life,* Robert Murphy tells the reader:

> The basic issue confronted by dialectical thought is the estrange-
> ment of man's existence. This estrangement arises from a di-
> lemma of both mind and external circumstance in which the
> unitary processes of human existence become fractured and
> broken into discrete entities by symbolization. The continuity,
> wholeness, and movement of the world of practical activity ap-
> pear in the world of thought, language, and culture as disconti-
> nuity, limitation, and fixity. What tends toward universality and
> oneness is broken into finite and opposed objects. (1971:87)

The models constructed by cultures give coherence to social life
by providing internally consistent frameworks of categories and
rules, rendered intelligible through related systems of meaning. The
structure described here is one such model. It is a complex and coherent syntax that structures much of social life, including brotherhood, marriage, spatial relationships, and exchange. Such structural
forms fix fluid experience.

The events of Northwest Amazon history run counter to the models of fixation and order. Historic experience in the upper Rio Negro
basin is one of dramatic upheavals, including enslavement, forced
migrations, and population decimation. The inconsistencies inherent in social relations, as well as the disturbances of history, become
fixed and reified in culture as structures. The early chapters on social organization focus on the structures of fixed identities of the
Wanano-Tukano, while the later chapters are concerned with the
fluidity of practical life. The elaborate set of rules regarding rank and
marriage would appear to fix the Wanano and other Eastern Tukanoans in an immutable web of prescription and social relations. Yet,
as the later chapters show, the rules as well as the categories are
mutable and responsive to historic circumstances.

Whereas the illusion of culture is permanence, the actuality of
practical life is absorption. Through open, yet stable, categories,
such as brotherhoods and alliances, the illusion of stability works to
structure different personnel and groups as they move into and
through these river basins over time. In the face of historic distur-
bance that threatens social integrity, an apparently inviolable order
is established that incorporates, absorbs, and orders difference.

The experience of history, then, so dissonant with an image of
order, is digested in the fixations of structure. The sources of sta-

bility, including the matrices of agnation and alliance, arrange mutual dependencies between groups, fixating and reifying these structures in performance and myth.

A culture's models effectively mystify the distinctions between history as enacted and history as represented. This is shown in the events recounted in chapter 10 when a junior sib accomplishes the monopolization of the important fishing weir of a dying senior sib. Neighboring senior sibs who might have challenged the claim fail to do so, emphasizing the absence of lateral ties between the seniors of different sib settlements. The junior group attempts to appropriate the past and the status of the dying seniors, to transform a *de facto* situation into a legitimate one. Key to the process is the necessity of forgetting, and the mystery and power in the continuity of name, regardless of the bearer. In time, the junior group will reconstruct a past and the status of the dying seniors; in so doing, one "history" will be forgotten, and another commemorated.

The events at Bucacopa, like those at Curideri, lend insight into the formation and repressions of structure. Each event may be understood as the intrusions of practical reality breaking apart a system and requiring its rectification. Yet the same historic sequence may be viewed as the source of vitality and continuity in the system. The incident at Bucacopa runs counter to the way things should be, the way they, in fact, have always been. It is an unrepresentable event, an "alternative" as opposed to an "official" history. The events at Bucacopa are the subversions of history and the making of it.

Appendix: Kin Terms

Simple Kin Terms for Wanano Referents

1. *nüchü.* FF, MF, FFB, MFB, FMZH, MMZH, MMB, FMB. All males ego's father calls *pükami* or *pükübü*. All male cognatic kin of the second ascending generation.

2. *nücho.* FM, MM, FMZ, MMZ, FFBW, MFBW, MFZ, FFZ. All female cognatic kin of the second ascending generation.

3. *pükü.* F.

4. *pükami.* FOB, and any kinsman father calls *wami*.

5. *pükübü.* FYB, and any kinsman father calls *büʔü*.

6. *wamanyo.* FZ, and any kinswoman father calls *wamio* or *baʔo*.

7. *wami.* OB, and the sons of all kinsmen father calls *wami*.

8. *büʔü.* YB, and the sons of all kinsmen father calls *büʔü*.

9. *wamio.* OZ, and the daughters of all kinsmen father calls *wami*.

10. *baʔo.* YZ, and the daughters of all kinsmen father calls *büʔü*.

11. *makü.* S, and the sons of all kinsmen male ego calls *wami* or *büʔü*.

12. *mako.* D, and the daughters of all kinsmen ego calls *wami* or *büʔü*.

13. *papükü.* Female ego only: BS, and the sons of all kinsmen female ego calls *wami* or *büʔü*.

14. *papüko.* Female ego only: BD, and the daughters of all kinsmen female ego calls *wami* or *büʔü*.

15. *panami.* All males of second descending generation.

16. *panamaio.* All females of second descending generation.

17. *wami makü/mako.* OBS, OBD.

18. *bü?ü makü/mako.* YBS, YBD.

Simple Kin Terms for Non-Wanano Referents

1. *püko.* M.

2. *bachü.* MB, FZH, and all persons mother calls *wami* or *bü?ü.*

3. *müonka.* MZ, FBW, and all persons mother calls *wamio* or *ba?o.*

4. *namo.* W.

5. *manu.* H.

6. *tanyü.* FZS, MBS, as well as the sons of all males mother calls *wami* or *bü?ü* or of the females father calls *wamio* or *ba?o.*

7. *tanyo.* FZD, MBD, as well as the daughters of all males mother calls *wami* or *bü?ü* or of the females father calls *wamio* or *ba?o.*

8. *buhibuo.* Male ego only: BW, as well as the wives of all persons ego calls *wami* or *bü?ü.*

9. *nasamo.* Female ego only: BW, as well as the wives of all persons female ego calls *wami* or *bü?ü.*

Compound Kin Terms for Non-Wanano Referents

1. *püko makü.* MZS when MZH is not classificatory FB.

2. *püko mako.* MZD when MZH is not classificatory FB.

3. *paka makü.* Male ego only: ZS and all sons of persons ego calls *wamio* or *ba?o.*

4. *paka mako.* Male ego only: ZD and all the daughters of persons ego calls *wamio* or *ba?o.*

5. *wamio makü.* OZS.

6. *wamio mako.* OZD.

7. *makü namono.* SW.

8. *wami namo.* OBW and wives of all men ego calls *wami.*

9. *bü?ü namo.* YBW and wives of all men ego calls *bü?ü.*

10. *namo makü.* WZS when WZH is not classificatory B.

11. *namo mako.* WZD when WZH is not classificatory B.

12. *tanyü makü.* MBSS or FZSS.

13. *tanyü mako.* MBSD or FZSD.

14. *tanyo makü.* MBDS or FZDS when MBD or FZD is not married to a Wanano.

15. *tanyo mako.* MBDD or FZDD when MBD or FZD is not married to a Wanano.

Note: The terms *nüchü, nücho, panami,* and *panamaio* include both Wanano and non-Wanano relatives.

Notes

Preface

1. Irving Goldman's *The Cubeo: Indians of the Northwest Amazon* (1963) was based upon fieldwork conducted in 1939.

2. I have given this village a fictitious name since some of the events described may be socially sensitive.

3. In the population census conducted by the Salesian Mission, sib name is used as last name. In this registry, the low-ranking family had reported themselves to be members of the high-ranking sib at Wapu. This family also sent their sons to the mission school to become teachers, to assume the prestige roles recently made available through mission education. These data, along with my own, suggest that while members of this sib publicly assumed the rank assigned them, they did not internalize the less prestigious social identity. Instead, they actively sought to acquire new statuses through opportunities made available through changing political environments.

1. Introduction

1. We were traveling to a National Women's Conference in Petrópolis, where we were invited speakers.

2. In Colombia, this river is spelled "Vaupés." I use the Portuguese spelling since the Wanano with whom I worked are located in Brazil.

3. Two principal towns in the Uaupés region, São Gabriel da Cachoeira in Brazil and Mitú in Colombia, are accessible by commercial air travel. From there access to the area is most feasible by small boat with outboard motor. The Brazilian Air Force (FAB) flies to the mission centers at Taracua, Pari Cachoeira, and Iauaretê; civilians are sometimes granted permission to travel on the planes.

4. The Cubeo (Goldman 1963) and Makuna (Århem 1981) are exceptions to the pattern of linguistic exogamy.

5. The named exogamous, descent groups of the Northwest Amazon have been referred to in the literature as "tribes" (Goldman 1963), "maximal exogamous units" (C. Hugh-Jones 1979; S. Hugh-Jones 1979); or "language

groups" (Jackson 1974). Goldman (1948) refers to the Cubeo as a "tribe" composed of smaller exogamous units or "phratries."

6. Sorensen then delineates four branches of the family: Tukano, Tuyuka, Yurutí, Paneroa, Eduria, Karapana, Tatuyo, and Barasana form one branch; Piratapuya and Wanano form a second branch; Desana and Siriano form a third branch; and Cubeo, alone, a fourth branch.

7. Eduardo Galvão identifies the Tariana, Baniwa, Tukano, Desana, Cubeo, and Makú groups in his Rio Negro subarea, and underestimates the total Uaupés population at 3,500 (1967: 187). The figure of 14,000 is reported by the Centro Ecumênico de Documentação e Informação (CEDI), Rio de Janeiro, 1990.

8. I discuss two principal language families here: the Arawakan and the Eastern Tukanoan. (The suffix -an indicates a language family as opposed to a single language group.) The Arawakan language groups I mention are the Tariana, the Baniwa, and a subgrouping of Baniwa known as the Curipaca. Aside from the Wanano, the Eastern Tukanoan groups I mention are the Desana, Cubeo, Tuyuka, Siriano, Piratapuya, and Tukano. In this text, "Tukanoan" or "Eastern Tukanoan" is used to refer to the body of language groups of the Eastern Tukanoan family and "Tukano," used alone, to refer to the group that speaks the language Tukano.

9. In other publications I have used the Brazilian spelling convention, "Uanano."

10. The upriver limit of Wanano occupation is said to be Uaracapury in Colombia (Waltz 1976). I did not visit the Colombian Wanano settlements.

11. Several sources estimate the Wanano population at between 100 and 250. For example, Joseph Grimes (1974) reports a population of about 250 for the Wanano. Darcy Ribeiro (1967: 157) estimates the "Wanana" population at between 100 and 250 and includes the Piratapuya as a subgroup. These figures were most likely based on Curt Nimuendajú's 1927 estimate of 218 (1950: 145). Although this census was conducted during a period of uncharacteristically low population density related to the destabilizing effects of the rubber boom following 1870, the figure has nevertheless recurred in the literature. Theodor Koch-Grünberg (1909), who visited the region in 1904, estimated the Wanano population to be between 500 and 600. Irving Goldman (1948: 765) and John Hemming (1978) both follow Koch-Grünberg in estimating the total Wanano population at close to 500 individuals.

12. The units of analysis I use range from the sib, a localized descent group; to a language group, comprised of sibs who share a common putative ancestor and speak one language; to the language family, comprised of related member language groups.

13. I selected the terms "chief" and "server" or "servant" in order to be consistent with studies on the Northwest Amazon where they are used (see, for example, C. Hugh-Jones, 1979). However, the meanings of these terms may not be isomorphic with the same terms used elsewhere. In the course of the book, the specific Northwest Amazon variants of these terms will become clear.

14. The concept of chiefdom that Carneiro utilizes derives from the work of Julian Steward (1948).

15. Compare this to Morton Fried: "Evolution of warfare and military statuses, at least during the earliest breakthroughs to more complex forms of society, followed and was dependent upon developments in technology, economic organization, and non-military aspects of social organization" (1967: 105–106; see also 185–186).

16. Christine and Stephen Hugh-Jones spent most of their time in a Barasana community on the Caño Colorado, but also visited Makuna, other Barasana, Bará, and Tatuyo of the upper Papurí.

2. European Expansion, Intertribal Relations, and Linguistic Exogamy in the Upper Rio Negro from 1616

1. In May 1624 the Dutch captured the capital of Brazil, Salvador da Bahia. Six years later a Dutch force captured the Pernambuco sites Olinda and Recife. The Portuguese regained these sites at great cost.

2. Other wood products taken from the forests of the upper Rio Negro were *carajurú* (a red dye), sarsaparilla, and *piaçaba* (a palm fiber used in the manufacture of brooms).

3. A *New York Times* report of February 9, 1991, describes an incident in which Venezuelan soldiers fired on a Brazilian pilot who thought he was in Brazil. Its author, James Brooke, writes that Brazil and Venezuela are "enmeshed in a dispute over the . . . 1,366 mile border."

4. Sir Walter Ralegh seems to have learned of this waterway during his first voyage to the Guianas in 1595, but its existence was not confirmed until Father Román's journey.

5. Koch-Grünberg (1909: 2:67) makes reference to a Wanano "chief" whose role appears to be symbolic and ceremonial. Since there are no data that connect these leadership functions to warfare, I do not consider him to be a "paramount chief" in the sense used here.

6. The ethnohistoric accounts discussed in this chapter were gathered in Wanano villages with frequent contact with in-law Arawakan Baniwa settlements on the Aiarí River. Oral histories and other ethnohistorical data were gathered from Wanano informants through taped interviews in Wanano, transcribed, and translated.

7. The sib is ideally a local descent group. While this is generally the case, a few settlements hold more than one sib, and some individuals live as "visitors" in the sib settlements of others.

8. In this text, "Tukanoan" or "Eastern Tukanoan" is used to refer to the body of language groups that comprise the Eastern Tukanoan family and "Tukano" to refer to the group that speaks the language Tukano.

9. All information on raiding practices, occurrences, and alliances is based on the recollections by older Wanano of stories told to them in their youth. The period to which informants referred is difficult to determine with much accuracy. I suspect that the contrast between the specificity that characterizes accounts of Baniwa advances and the lack of specificity asso-

ciated with Tariana advances indicates a difference in the period in question. Historic accounts from 1730 place the Tariana at the mouth of the Uaupés. These events are discussed in greater detail in Chernela 1983.

10. Named groups said to have been defended with spiked trenches were the Bu?sa Dita and the Wipi Pona sibs. Goldman (1963) also reports spiked trenches for Cubeo settlements on the northern affluents of the Uaupés adjacent to Baniwa territories.

11. The suffix *-pona*, "children of," is the conventional means of referring to a Tukanoan sib.

12. Nyapia Taro Pona, meaning "Children of the Stars," is the Wanano name for the Baniwa Wari Peri (also known as Siusi) sib, located along the Aiarí, Cuduiarí, and Içana rivers.

13. The Wipi Pona settlements, like the Bu?sa Dita settlements, were defended by spiked trenches.

14. Robin Wright (1981) and William McGovern (1927) agree that these locations were seized by the Tariana from former Tukanoan inhabitants. Arthur Sorensen (pers. com., August 4, 1990) finds the same degree of detail in recollections of settlement displacement he gathered on the Uaupés and Papurí. His data also support displacement of Eastern Tukanoan settlements by Tariana on the lower and middle Uaupés.

15. Wanano critically observed that the Baniwa Wayu Pona fought among themselves, revealing their own prohibitions on hostilities among brother groups.

3. Scientific and Missionary Activities in the Uaupés Basin from 1760

1. Koch-Grünberg (1909: 8) calls Frei Gregorio de Bene a Carmelite padre (unlike Bruzzi [1977] and Wright [1981], who describe him as Capuchin).

2. All passages from Koch-Grünberg cited here were translated from the German by Jill Bauer.

3. These were Querarí at the mouth of the tributary of the same name, Uaracapury on the cascades of the same name, Macaquinha, Micurigarapaua, and Mutúm.

4. Social Organization

1. The Cubeo (Goldman 1963) and Makuna (Århem 1981) are exceptions to the pattern of linguistic exogamy.

2. I choose the term "language group" rather than using Christine and Stephen Hugh-Jones' term, the "simple" or "maximal exogamous unit." While the latter terms are extremely precise, I prefer the straightforward qualities of the first. Whenever possible, I have tried to avoid the terms "tribe" and "subtribe" used by Arthur Sorensen (1967) and Irving Goldman (1963) for reasons described by Morton Fried (1975).

3. Since some settlements consist of two sections, the number might be higher by a different calculation.

4. The exceptional case of the Wiroa, or "slave" Wanano, is discussed below.

5. In high-ranked villages, an attempt is made to attract "visitors" who are obligated to perform services in order to reside there. For example, the highest-ranked sib, the Biari Pona, invited a full in-law sib, a "servant" Wanano sib, and a "client" Maku sib (see chapter 10). In Yapima (second in rank), the two highest-ranked males had resident client sons-in-law performing services for them and the community. They invited a Wanano "servant" sib to occupy a hamlet within their environs and called upon them when laborious tasks were performed.

6. The importance of this was shown in a rare case of linguistic endogamy I encountered that involved two members of a Wanano affine group, the Tukano. Having moved to a city, the couple apparently felt free of the linguistic exogamy regulation and married. The final explanation that circulated in the Uaupés area to account for the heresy was that the groom, having been raised outside the region, never received his "breath" name and was therefore "not a Tukano." Not having a "breath" name, he had no social affiliation.

7. I use the generic masculine when it characterizes the Wanano viewpoint. It must be remembered that this is a patrilineal system in which group identity is derived from the father.

8. The relation between the *mahsa wami* and his fellow sib-mates and villagers is discussed in chapter 9.

9. "Class" is used here in the general sense of category.

10. The preferred practice of cross-cousin marriage has significant implications in terms of language usage. If a man marries his father's sister's daughter, he is assured a spouse whose mother speaks his own language; with a mother's-brother's-daughter marriage, a man is assured a wife whose own language is the same as his mother's.

11. In later marriages, expediency is given primary consideration. This sometimes creates a dilemma, as shown later. Preference applies only to first marriages.

12. The following abbreviations are used in discussing kinship nomenclature: F = father, M = mother, B = brother, Z = sister, S = son, D = daughter, H = husband, W = wife, O = older, Y = younger. Thus, the letters FZS, FZD, MBS, and MBD stand for father's sister's son, father's sister's daughter, mother's brother's son, and mother's brother's daughter, respectively.

13. In this context, *tanyo* has been translated as "cousin."

5. Kinship Nomenclature

1. Several researchers refer to this pattern of kinship classification as Dravidian, following L. H. Morgan's worldwide compilation of kinship terminologies. Using the Tamil case as representative of Dravidian languages, Morgan listed as many as twenty-three distinctive features of this type. He noted its similarity to the Iroquois type and included them in the same

"Classificatory" class, but distinguished the two principally on the basis of differences in the first descending generation: in the Dravidian system, children of same-sex cross-cousins are cross-cousins to one another, whereas children of opposite sex cross-cousins are equated with *own* children. Morgan (and later Rivers 1968) concluded that this was the consequence of the practice of ongoing cross-cousin marriage. There has been debate about the appropriateness of the term "Dravidian" for this pattern; recently Gertrude Dole (1983, 1991) devised the name "Cross-Cousin" for the type (Morgan 1871: 387, note 1).

6. Gender, Language, and Placement in Wanano Poetic Forms

1. Sorensen 1967, Jackson 1983, C. Hugh-Jones 1979, S. Hugh-Jones 1979, and others report similar findings for other Eastern Tukanoan groups.

2. In Wanano, there is no distinction between the words "soul" and "heart" as they are used here. I have alternated the words in translation to satisfy conventions in English.

7. The Succulence of Place: Control and Distribution of Fish Resources

1. Chernela 1989a contains a more detailed discussion of blackwater ecosystems.

2. For a full discussion of neotropical margin types, see Prance 1979.

3. The plural "fish" is used here for the general mass, for multiple fish of a single species, and for the food, while "fishes" is used to indicate a collective containing more than one species.

4. Data are based on 1,910 fishing man-hours, in which location was recorded for every fish captured. Approximately 80 fishing locations were classified into the following habitat types: (1) seasonally flooded forests; (2) cataracts; (3) river margin (of unknown type); (4) island point; (5) sand beach; (6) *terra firme* upland; and (7) unknown.

5. Fishing data were gathered between December 1978 and November 1979. Two families were selected for intense study: their fishing and consumption activities were followed on a daily basis for nearly the full period. In addition, the activities of 25 fishermen were observed sporadically to verify typicality, to assemble a sample that would provide a significant number of cases, and to broaden the range of fishing methods considered. Periodic rounds were also made to all of the settlement's households at dawn (when fish is prepared and eaten) to record the comparative fishing catches of the previous night. These visits provided most of the catches recorded for the 25 fishermen. In this way, 1,910 fishing hours were recorded. For each reported yield of fish, the following data were collected: name of fisherman; number of fishers in party; departure time; return time; method of capture; location of capture; method of preparation; time of consumption; age of consumers; and relationship of consumers to fisherman. Each fish was weighed, measured, and examined for certain biological features, such as eggs or parasites. Fishing zones were visited and classified

according to habitat. I took part in numerous fishing trips and conducted interviews on fishing methods. In addition, I assembled a sample collection of over 200 fishes for identification and deposit at the Instituto Nacional de Pesquisas de Amazonia (INPA), the Museu de Zoologia of São Paulo, and the Museu Goeldi, Belêm. Identifications were made by ichthyologists at these institutions, as well as at the Smithsonian Institution's Department of Fishes, where tentative identifications were made on the basis of polychrome slides. The fishes in the sample collection were captured using nets provided by INPA and the Smithsonian Institution Museum of Natural History. The use of nets for samples also provided a basis for comparison with traditional methods.

6. Kathleen Clark (1982) reports widespread use of drag-lines in the San Carlos area of Venezuela, where the necessary equipment is more accessible.

8. The *Po?oa* Exchange

1. Specialized crafts are not subject to such environmental factors.

2. This "exchange relay" shows the advantage of access to a Makú group.

3. Before issuing such invitations, the Wanano sib first had to obtain the approval of their Desana in-laws. These data suggest that Wanano access to Makú labor is a significant advantage in Desana co-residence.

4. The beer in one relatively small vessel, containing 9 kg of beer, requires 20 man-hours of active labor and 55 total hours to produce.

5. Marshall Sahlins' point that "in primitive society social inequality is more the organization of economic equality" appears to be borne out (1972: 205).

9. Rank and Leadership within a Wanano Settlement

1. The names in this chapter, including Curideri, are fictitious.

2. Anthropologists only recently have begun to examine the effects of missionary work on indigenous cultures. In 1970, Elmer Miller described a "breakdown" in Toba traditional ideology as a result of mission influence. Edward Schieffelin (1981) documented the dramatic reorientation of the primary Kaluli reciprocal mode of organizing both social and economic relations as a result of mission activity; this change, despite its pervasive nature, took place in only eight years. These papers (along with those of Beidelman 1974; Shapiro 1981; Wright 1981; and others) form the important groundwork from which a body of literature on missionization is now developing.

10. The Bucacopa Case: Rank and Obligation among Three Uaupés Sibs

1. Although Desana are found on the main Uaupés living among in-laws, there are no Desana settlements there. Furthermore, unlike the Wa-

nano, the Desana hunt a fair amount. These and other observations suggest that the Desana are traditional inhabitants of the forest interior or the headwaters of tributaries, areas where Wanano do not venture. The differences between the Desana and other Uaupés groups merit further investigation.

2. Koch-Grünberg remarks on the Makú at Bucacopa in 1904 (1909: 2:59–60).

3. The case of Nicho illustrates the degree to which a woman's allegiances are divided. At least in her case, the bonds between Nicho and her affines were closer than her bonds to her junior kin.

4. I have called this a "second song" because it follows an interruption. It may be a continuation of the first song.

5. Nicho's son is also her sister's husband's brother's son.

11. Conclusion

1. There are numerous versions of this origin myth. Some refer to several ancestral anacondas (see, for example, Århem 1981 and C. Hugh-Jones 1979).

References Cited

Aranha, Bento de Figueiredo Tenreiro (ed.)
  1907   Archivo do Amazonas. *Revista Destinada a Vulgarisação de Do-
           cumentos Geográficos e Históricos do Estado do Amazonas* 1 (3).
Århem, Kaj
  1981   *Makuna Social Organization: A Study in Descent, Alliance, and
           the Formation of Corporate Groups in the North-Western Ama-
           zon.* Uppsala Studies in Cultural Anthropology 4. Stockholm:
           Almqvist & Wiksell.
  1989   "The Maku, the Makuna, and the Guiana System: Transforma-
           tions of Social Structure in Northern Lowland South America."
           Ethnos (1–2): 5–22.
Beidelman, Thomas O.
  1974   "Social Theory and the Study of Christian Mission in Africa."
           Africa 44(3): 235–249.
Boxer, Charles R.
  1962   *The Golden Age of Brazil.* Berkeley, Cal.: University of Califor-
           nia Press.
Bruzzi Alves da Silva, P. Alcionilio
  1977   *A Civilização Indígena do Uaupés,* 2nd ed. Missão Salesiana do
           Rio Negro, Amazonas, Brazil.
Carneiro, Robert L.
  1970   "A Theory of the Origin of the State." *Science* 169:733–738.
  1981   "The Chiefdom: Precursor of the State." In *The Transition to
           Statehood in the New World,* ed. Grant Jones and Robert Krautz,
           pp. 37–79. New York: Cambridge University Press.
  1987   "Further Reflections on Resource Concentration and its Role in
           the Rise of the State." In *Studies in the Neolithic and Urban
           Revolutions,* ed. Linda Manzanilla, pp. 245–260. BAR Interna-
           tional Series 349. Oxford: BAR.
  1990   "Chiefdom Level Warfare as Exemplified in Fiji and the Cauca
           Valley." In *The Anthropology of War,* ed. Jonathon Haas, pp. 190–
           211. Cambridge: Cambridge University Press.
  1991   "The Nature of the Chiefdom as Revealed by Evidence from the

Cauca Valley of Colombia." In *Profiles in Cultural Evolution,* ed.
A. Terry Rambo and Kathleen Gillogly, pp. 167–190. Anthropological Papers No. 85. Ann Arbor: University of Michigan Museum of Anthropology.

Carvajal, Gaspar de
1941   *Descobrimentos do Rio das Amazonas.* São Paulo: Editora Nacional. Portuguese translation of the author's *Descubrimiento
del Río de las Amazonas,* Edición de Sevilla, 1894.

Chernela, Janet M.
1982a   "Estrutura Social do Uaupés Brasileiro." *Anuário Antropológico/
81,* ed. Roberto Cardoso de Oliveria (Rio de Janeiro) 81:59–69.
1982b   "An Indigenous System of Forest and Fisheries Management in
the Uaupés Basin of Brazil." *Cultural Survival Quarterly,* 6(2):
17–18.
1983   "Hierarchy and Economy of the Uanano (Kotiria) Speaking
Peoples of the Middle Uaupés Basin." Ph.D. dissertation, Columbia University. University Microfilms International, Ann Arbor.
1985a   "Indigenous Fishing in the Neotropics: The Tukanoan Uanano of
the Blackwater Uaupés River Basin in Brazil and Colombia." *Interciência,* 10(2): 78–86.
1985b   "Why One Culture Stays Put: A Case of Resistance to Change in
Authority and Economic Structure in an Indigenous Community
in the Northwest Amazon." In *Change in the Amazon Basin,*
Volume 2: *The Frontier after a Decade of Colonisation,* ed.
John Hemming, pp. 228–236. Manchester: Manchester University Press.
1987   "Endangered Ideologies: Tukano Fishing Taboos." *Cultural Survival Quarterly* 11(2): 50–52.
1988a   "Gender, Language and 'Placement' in Uanano Songs and Litanies." *Journal of Latin American Lore* 14(2): 193–206.
1988b   "Righting History in the Northwest Amazon." In *Rethinking
History and Myth,* ed. Jonathan Hill, pp. 35–49. Urbana/Chi-
cago: University of Illinois Press.
1988c   "Some Considerations of Myth and Gender." In *Dialectics and
Gender: Anthropological Approaches,* ed. Richard Randolph and
David Schneider, pp. 67–79. Boulder/London: Westview Press.
1989a   "Managing Rivers of Hunger: The Importance of the Blackwater
River Margin." In *Resource Management in Amazonia: Indigenous and Folk Strategies,* ed. William Balee and Darrell Posey,
pp. 238–248. Advances in Economic Botany, 7. New York: New
York Botanical Garden.
1989b   "Marriage, Language, and History among Eastern Tukanoan
Speaking Peoples of the Northwest Amazon." *Latin American
Anthropology Review* 1(2): 36–42.
1992   "Social Meanings and Material Transaction: The Wanano-
Tukano of Brazil and Colombia." *Journal of Anthropological Ar-
chaeology* (11): 111–124.

Clark, Kathleen
  1982 "Subsistence Fishing at San Carlos de Rio Negro, Venezuela." Unpublished manuscript.
Codazzi, Giovanni Battista Agostino
  1940 *Resumen de la Geografía de Venezuela (Venezuela en 1841).* 3 vols. Vol. 2. Caracas: Taller de Artes Gráficas. Escuela Técnica Industrial.
Coudreau, Henri A.
  1887 "Voyage à travers les Guyanes et l'Amazonie." *La France Equinoxiale.* Vol. 2. Paris: Challamel.
Dole, Gertrude
  1983 "Some Aspects of Structure in Kuikuru Society." Unpublished manuscript.
  1991 "The Development of Kinship in Tropical South America." In *Profiles in Cultural Evolution: Papers from a Conference in Honor of Elman R. Service.* ed. A. Terry Rambo and Kathleen Gillogly, Anthropological Papers No. 85, pp. 373–403. Ann Arbor: University of Michigan Museum of Anthropology.
Earle, Timothy K.
  1977 "A Reappraisal of Redistribution: Complex Hawaiian Chiefdoms." In *Exchange Systems in Prehistory,* ed. Timothy K. Earle and Jonathon E. Ericson, pp. 213–228. New York: Academic Press.
Fried, Morton H.
  1960 "On the Evolution of Social Stratification and the State." In *Culture in History, Essay in Honor of Paul Radin,* ed. Stanley Diamond, pp. 713–721. New York: Published for Brandeis University by Columbia University Press.
  1967 *The Evolution of Political Society: An Essay in Political Anthropology.* New York: Random House.
  1975 *The Notion of Tribe.* Menlo Park, Cal.: Cummings Publishing Company.
Galvão, Eduardo
  1967 "Indigenous Culture Areas of Brazil, 1900–1959." In *Indians of Brazil in the Twentieth Century,* ed. Janice H. Hopper, pp. 169–205. ICR Studies 2. Washington, D.C.: Institute for Cross-Cultural Research.
Geisler, R., H. A. Knoppel, and H. Sioli
  1973 "The Ecology of Freshwater Fishes in Amazonia: Present Status and Future Tasks for Research." In *Applied Sciences and Development,* 2:144–162. Tübingen: Institute for Scientific Cooperation.
Goldman, Irving
  1948 "Tribes of the Uaupés-Caqueta Region." In *Handbook of South American Indians* 3:763–798. Washington, D.C.: Smithsonian Institution.
  1955 "Status Rivalry and Cultural Evolution in Polynesia." *American Anthropologist* 57:680–697.

1957　"Variations in Polynesian Social Organization." *Journal of the Polynesian Society* 66(4): 374–390.

1963　*The Cubeo: Indians of the Northwest Amazon.* Illinois Studies in Anthropology, no. 2. Urbana: University of Illinois Press.

1981　"Foundations of Social Hierarchy: A Northwest Amazon Case." Paper presented to the New York Academy of Sciences, February 23, 1981.

Goulding, M.

1980　*The Fishes and the Forest.* Berkeley: University of California Press.

Grimes, Joseph E.

1974　*Word Lists and Languages.* Ithaca, N.Y.: Cornell University.

Hemming, John

1978　*Red Gold: The Conquest of the Brazilian Indians.* Cambridge, Mass.: Harvard University Press.

Hill, Jonathan

1983　"Wakuenai Society: A Processual-Structural Analysis of Indigenous Cultural Life in the Upper Rio Negro Basin, Venezuela." Ph.D. dissertation, Indiana University. University Microfilms International, Ann Arbor.

1984　"Social Equality and Ritual Hierarchy: The Arawakan Wakuenai of Venezuela." *American Ethnologist* 11: 528–544.

Hopper, Janice H.

1967　*Indians of Brazil in the Twentieth Century.* Washington, D.C.: Institute for Cross-Cultural Research.

Hugh-Jones, Christine

1979　*From the Milk River: Spatial and Temporal Processes in Northwest Amazonia.* Cambridge: Cambridge University Press.

Hugh-Jones, Stephen

1979　*The Palm and the Pleiades: Initiation and Cosmology in Northwest Amazonia.* Cambridge: Cambridge University Press.

Humboldt, Alexander von, and Aimé Bonpland

1852　*Personal Narrative of Travels to the Equinoctial Regions of America during the Years 1799–1804.* 3 vols. Translated and edited by Thomasina Ross. Vol. 2. London: Henry G. Bohn.

Hynes, H. B.

1970　*Ecology of Running Waters.* Toronto: University of Toronto Press.

Jackson, Jean E.

1972　"Marriage and Linguistic Identity among the Bará Indians of the Vaupés, Colombia." Ph.D. dissertation, Stanford University.

1974　"Language Identity of the Colombian Vaupés Indians." In *Explorations in the Ethnography of Speaking,* ed. R. Bauman and J. Sherzer, pp. 50–64. Cambridge: Cambridge University Press.

1976　"Vaupés Marriage: A Network System in an Undifferentiated Lowland Area of South America." In *Regional Analysis,* vol. 2: *Social Systems,* ed. C. Smith, pp. 65–93. New York: Academic Press.

1977   "Bará Zero-generation Terminology and Marriage." *Ethnology* 16(1): 83–104.

1983   *The Fish People: Linguistic Exogamy and Tukanoan Identity in Northwest Amazonia.* New York: Cambridge University Press.

Kirchoff, Paul
1955   "The Principles of Clanship in Human Society." *Davidson Journal of Anthropology* 1(1): 1–10.

Knoppel, H. A.
1970   "Food of Central Amazonian Fishes: Contribution to the Nutrient-ecology of Amazonian Rain-forest Streams." *Amazoniana* 2(3): 257–352.

Koch-Grünberg, Theodor
1909   *Zwei Jahre unter den Indianern: Reisen in nordwest-Brasilien 1903/1905,* 2 vols. Berlin: Ernst Wasmuth.

Leach, E. R.
1954   *Political Systems of Highland Burma: A Study of Kachin Social Structure.* Monographs on Social Anthropology, no. 44. London: London School of Economics.

Lévi-Strauss, Claude
1969   *The Elementary Structures of Kinship.* Translated by J. H. Bell and J. R. von Sturmer; edited by R. Needham. Boston: Beacon Press.

Malinowski, Bronislaw
1922   *Argonauts of the Western Pacific.* London: Routledge and Kegan Paul.

Marlier, G.
1967   "Hydrobiology in the Amazon Region." *Atas do Simpósio sobre a Biota Amazônica* ser. 3: 1–7.

Martius, Karl Friedrich Philipp von
1867   *Beiträge zur Ethnographie und Sprachenkunde Amerika's zumal Braziliens.* Leipzig: F. Fleischer.

Massa, Dom Pedro
1933   *Pelo Rio Mar.* Rio de Janeiro.

McGovern, William
1927   *Jungle Paths and Inca Ruins.* London: Hutchinson.

Meggers, Betty
1971   *Amazonia: Man and Culture in a Counterfeit Paradise.* Chicago: Aldine.

Miller, Elmer S.
1970   "The Christian Missionary, Agent of Secularization." *Anthropological Quarterly* 43(1): 14–22.

Ministério das Minas e Energia
1976   *Projeto Radambrasil: Levantamento de Recursos Naturais.* Vol. 11. Rio de Janeiro.

Morgan, L. H.
1871   *Systems of Consanguinity and Affinity of the Human Family.* Smithsonian Contributions to Knowledge, vol. 17, no. 218. Washington, D.C.: Smithsonian Institution.

Murdock, George Peter
  1951   "South American Culture Areas." *Southwestern Journal of Anthropology* 4:415–436.
Murphy, Robert F.
  1961   "Deviance and Social Control I: What Makes Waru Run?" *Kroeber Anthropological Society Papers* 24:55–61.
  1971   *The Dialectics of Social Life.* New York: Columbia University Press.
  1986   *Cultural and Social Anthropology: An Overture.* 2nd ed. Englewood Cliffs, N.J.: Prentice-Hall.
Nimuendajú, Curt
  1950   "Reconhecimento dos Rios Içana, Ayari, e Uaupés: Relatório apresentado ão Serviço de Proteção ãos Índios do Amazonas de Acre, 1927." *Journal de la Société des Américanistes* 39 (Paris): 125–182.
Ortner, Sherry
  1975   "God's Bodies, God's Food: A Symbolic Analysis of a Sherpa Ritual." In *The Interpretation of Symbolism,* ed. Roy Willis, pp. 133–169. New York: Wiley.
Peebles, Christopher, and Susan M. Kus
  1977   "Some Archaeological Correlates of Ranked Societies." *American Antiquity* 42:521–548.
Piddocke, Stuart
  1965   "The Potlatch System of the Southern Kwakiutl: A New Perspective." *Southwestern Journal of Anthropology* 21:244–264.
Prance, G. T.
  1979   "Notes on the Vegetation of Amazonia III: The Terminology of Amazonian Forest Types Subject to Inundation." *Brittonia* 31(1): 26–38.
Ramos, Alcida Rita, Peter Silverwood-Cope, and Ana Gita de Oliveira
  1980   "Patrões e Clientes: Relações Intertribais no Alto Rio Negro." In *Hierarquia e Simbiose: Relações Intertribais no Brasil,* ed. Alcida Rita Ramos, pp. 135–182. São Paulo: Editora Hucitec em convênio com o Instituto Nacional do Livro, Ministério da Educação e Cultura.
Ramos Pérez, Demetrio
  1946   *El Tratado de Límites de 1750 y la Expedición de Iturriaga al Orinoco.* Madrid: Consejo Superior de Investigaciones Científicas, Instituto Juan Sebastián Elcano.
Reichel-Dolmatoff, Gerardo
  1971   *Amazonian Cosmos: The Sexual and Religious Symbolism of the Tukano Indians.* Chicago: University of Chicago Press. (Originally published as *Desana, Simbolismo de los Indios Tucano del Vaupés;* Bogota: Universidad de los Andes, 1968.)
  1975   *The Shaman and the Jaguar.* Philadelphia: Temple University Press.

1979   "Cosmology as Ecological Analysis: A View from the Rainforest." *Man* 2(3): 207–318.

Reid, Howard
1979   "Some Aspects of Movement, Growth and Change among the Hupdu Maku." Ph.D. dissertation, Cambridge University.

Ribeiro, Darcy
1967   "Indigenous Cultures and Languages of Brazil." In *Indians of Brazil in the Twentieth Century*, ed. Janice H. Hopper, pp. 77–165. ICR Studies 2. Washington, D.C.: Institute for Cross-Cultural Research.

Rivers, W. H. R.
1968   *Kinship and Social Organization.* London School of Economics Monograph on Social Anthropology no. 34. London: Athlone Press.

Roberts, T. R.
1972   "Ecology of Fishes in the Amazon and Congo Basins." *Bulletin of the Museum of Comparative Zoology*, 143(2): 117–147.

Rondón, Gen. Frederico
1969   *Pelos Sertões e Fronteiras do Brasil.* Rio de Janeiro: Reper Editora.

Sahlins, Marshall
1958   *Social Stratification in Polynesia.* Seattle: University of Washington Press.

1972   *Stone Age Economics.* Chicago: Aldine.

1981   *Historical Metaphors and Mythical Realities: Structure in the Early History of the Sandwich Islands Kingdom.* Association for Social Anthropology in Oceania. Ann Arbor: University of Michigan Press.

Salati, Eneas, Jose Marquez, and Luis Carlos B. Molion
1978   "Origem e Distribuição das Chuvas na Amazonia." *Interciência* 3(4): 200–206.

Santos, U. de Menezes, S. R. Bulção Bringel, H. Bergamin Filho, M. de Nazaré Góes Ribeiro, and M. Bananeira
1984   "Rios da Bacia Amazônica I: Afluentes do Rio Negro." *Acta Amazônica* 14(1–2): 222–237.

Schieffelin, Edward L.
1981   "Evangelical Rhetoric and the Transformation of Traditional Culture in Papua New Guinea." *Comparative Studies in Society and History*, 23(1): 150–156.

Schmidt, G. W.
1969   "Vertical Distribution of Bacteria and Algae in a Tropical Lake." *Int. Rev. Ges. Hydrobiol.*: 791–797.

1970   "Number of Bacteria and Algae and Their Interrelations in Some Amazonia Waters." *Amazoniana* 2: 393–400.

1973a   "Primary Production of Phytoplankton in the Three Types of Amazonia Waters, 2." *Amazoniana* 4(2): 139–203.

1973b   "Primary Productivity of Phytoplankton in a Tropical Floodplain

Lake of Central Amazonia." *Amazoniana* 4:379–404.
1976   "Primary Production of Phytoplankton in the Three Types of Amazonia Waters, 4." *Amazoniana* 5(4): 517–528.
Service, Elman R.
1962   *Primitive Social Organization: An Evolutionary Perspective.* New York: Random House.
Shapiro, Judith
1981   "Ideologies of Catholic Missionary Practice in a Postcolonial Era." *Comparative Studies in Society and History*, 23(1): 130–149.
Silverwood-Cope, Peter
1972   "A Contribution to the Ethnography of the Colombian Maku." Ph.D. dissertation, Cambridge University.
Sioli, H.
1968   "Principal Biotypes of Primary Production in the Waters of Amazonia. In *Proceedings of the Symposium on Recent Advances in Tropical Ecology*, ed. R. Misra and B. Gopal, pp. 591–600. Varanasi: International Society for Tropical Ecology.
1975   "Tropical River: The Amazon." In *River Ecology*, ed. B. A. Whitton, pp. 461–488. Berkeley: University of California Press.
Smith, Nigel
1981   *Man, Fishes and the Amazon.* New York: Columbia University Press.
Soares, Maria Gercilia Mota
1979   "Aspectos ecológicos (alimentação e reprodução) dos peixes do Igarapé do Porto, Aripuana, M. T." *Acta Amazônica* 9(2): 325–352.
Sorensen, Arthur P., Jr.
1967   "Multilingualism in the Northwest Amazon." *American Anthropologist* 69:670–684.
1969   "The Morphology of Tukano." Ph.D. dissertation, Columbia University.
Sousa, (Marechal) Boanerges Lopes de
1959   Do Rio Negro ão Orenoco. A Terra—O Homem. No. 111. Rio de Janeiro: Conselho Nacional de Proteção ãos Indios.
Souza, Conego André Fernandes de
1848   Notícias Geográficas da Capitanía de São José do Rio Negro. *Revista do Instituto Histórico Geográfico Brasileiro* 10:411–504.
Spruce, R.
1908   *Notes of a Botanist on the Amazon and Andes.* 2 vols. London: Macmillan.
Steward, Julian
1948   *Handbook of South American Indians.* Vol. 3. Washington, D.C.: Smithsonian Institution.
Steward, Julian H., and Louis C. Faron
1959   *Native Peoples of South America.* New York: McGraw-Hill.

Suttles, Wayne
  1960   "Affinal Ties, Subsistence, and Prestige among the Coast Salish."
          American Anthropologist 62:296–305.
Sweet, David G.
  1974   "A Rich Realm of Nature Destroyed: The Middle Amazon Valley
          1640–1750." Ph.D. dissertation, University of Wisconsin. Uni-
          versity Microfilms International, Ann Arbor.
Vayda, Andrew P.
  1961   "A Re-examination of Northwest Coast Economic Systems."
          Transactions of the New York Academy of Sciences Ser. 2, no.
          23:618–624.
Wallace, Alfred Russel
  1969   *A Narrative of Travels on the Amazon and Rio Negro.* 2nd ed.,
          New York: Haskell House. (originally published London, 1870).
Waltz, Nathan
  1976   Hablemos el Guanano: Gramática Pedagógica Guanano-Caste-
          llano. Bogotá: Ministerio de Gobierno, División Operativa de
          Asuntos Indígenas. Instituto Lingüístico de Verano.
Waltz, Nathan, and Carolyn Waltz
  1980   "Notes on Guanano Kinship." Ms., Summer Institute of Linguis-
          tics, Bogotá.
  n.d.   Fonología del Guanano. Bogotá: Instituto Lingüístico de Verano.
Welcomme, R. L.
  1979   *Fisheries Ecology of Floodplain Rivers.* New York: Longman.
Wright, Robin
  1981   "History and Religion of the Baniwa Peoples of the Upper Rio
          Negro Valley." Ph.D. dissertation, Stanford University.

Index